PEAK DISTRICT WALKING
– On·The Level –

Norman Buckley

Published by Sigma Leisure – an imprint of
Sigma Press, 5 Alton Road, Wilmslow, Cheshire SK9 5DY, England.

British Library Cataloguing in Publication Data
A CIP record for this book is available from the British Library.

ISBN: 1-85058-811-2

Typesetting and Design by: Sigma Press, Wilmslow, Cheshire.

Maps: created by Jeremy Semmens and jngendy and from Ordnance Survey based mapping on behalf of The Controller of Her Majesty's Stationery Office © Crown Copyright 2004 100032058

Photographs: Norman Buckley

Cover: main picture The Monsal Trail; small pictures, from top – Three Shire Heads; Ashford-in-the-Water; countryside scene

Printed by: Interprint Ltd.

Disclaimer: the information in this book is given in good faith and is believed to be correct at the time of publication. No responsibility is accepted by either the author or publisher for errors or omissions, or for any loss or injury howsoever caused. Only you can judge your own fitness, competence and experience.

Preface

This book, the fifth volume of the well-established 'level walk' series, covers the Peak District, an immensely popular area, mostly within Britain's first National Park. Routes among the hills, plateaux and steep-sided valleys have challenged generations of enthusiastic walkers.

However, it is the author's belief that there are many more walkers and potential walkers who could and would enjoy this superb countryside if attractive routes could be found which guarantee the minimum ascent, good conditions underfoot and an assured return to the starting place. The earlier volumes, dealing with the Lake District (two), Yorkshire Dales and North Wales, have proved that, for a variety of reasons, not all countryside lovers have the ability and/or the desire to make the effort required to climb to the hilltops or other high places.

The term 'level' in the title is not, of course, to be taken literally. Very few walks could meet this criterion; even the designated trails using former railway lines do have gradients! It does indicate that, in selecting and examining routes for possible inclusion, the first consideration is always the ascent, both in total and in the length and steepness of particular sections.

Almost by definition, 'level' walks are likely also to be comparatively short walks. However, the twenty-eight mainly circular routes included in this book cover a wide variety of terrain, ranging from the splendours of Dovedale and the wild moorland above Froggatt Edge to the gentle surroundings of Tittensor and the beautiful Derwent riverside.

Good footpaths, bridleways and lanes are always the first choice; scrambling over rock and excessively muddy areas are avoided. Sections of road are included only when unavoidable for the completion of a circuit.

The format setting out each walk provides 'at a glance' introductory information, which is intended to help the reader select a walk more easily. As walking speeds are very variable, no estimated times are given. Three kilometres (two miles) per hour is about average, allowing time for occasional stops for photography and informal refreshment, but not for picnics. As 'level' walking is a leisurely occupation, refreshment opportunities are given in all appropriate cases, together with information on features of likely interest.

The combination of detailed route directions and a sketch map is adequate for the successful completion of each walk. Nevertheless, possession of a large-scale (1:25,000) detailed map does add greatly to the appreciation of the landscape. The Peak District is fully covered by Ordnance Survey Explorer OL1, The Peak District, Dark Peak area and OL24, The Peak District, White Peak area. Both these maps were formerly part of the Outdoor Leisure series. Whilst for comparatively gentle walks it is hardly necessary to have elaborate 'mountain' clothing and equipment, most walkers feel more comfortable, whatever the weather conditions, if they are adequately shod and have extra clothing, including waterproofs.

Norman Buckley

Contents

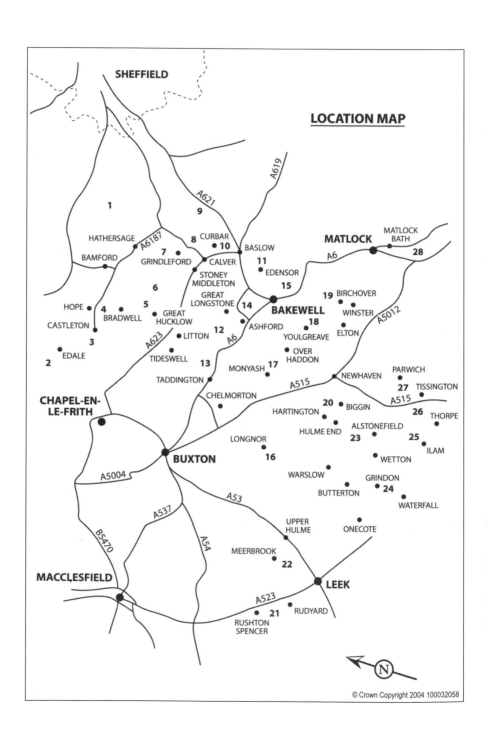

LOCATION MAP

SHEFFIELD

A619

A621

1

9

HATHERSAGE

A6187

8 CURBAR
● 10

BASLOW

MATLOCK

MATLOCK
BATH

BAMFORD

7
GRINDLEFORD

CALVER

11 EDENSOR
●

A6

28

STONEY
MIDDLETON

6

GREAT
LONGSTONE

15

BIRCHOVER
19

HOPE ●

5

14

BAKEWELL

WINSTER

A5012

4 BRADWELL

GREAT
HUCKLOW

ASHFORD

18

CASTLETON

3

12
LITTON

A6

YOULGREAVE

ELTON

EDALE
2

A623

TIDESWELL

13

OVER
HADDON

MONYASH 17

NEWHAVEN

PARWICH

27 TISSINGTON

TADDINGTON

A515

A515

CHAPEL-EN-
LE-FRITH

CHELMORTON

20 BIGGIN

26 THORPE

HARTINGTON

ALSTONEFIELD
23

25 ILAM

LONGNOR

HULME END

WETTON

BUXTON

16

WARSLOW

GRINDON
24

A5004

BUTTERTON

WATERFALL

A53

UPPER
HULME

ONECOTE

A537

MEERBROOK

B5470

22

A54

MACCLESFIELD

LEEK

A523

21 RUDYARD

RUSHTON
SPENCER

N

© Crown Copyright 2004 100032058

Introduction

The Peak District is well-placed at the division between the north and south of the country: between the hillier, more remote and generally colder north and the flatter, softer and warmer south. It is readily accessible to visitors from far and wide, and is the most visited National Park in the country. In particular, it has long been a favoured playground for those residents of the great conurbations such as Manchester, Leeds/Bradford, Sheffield and the Potteries, who value the countryside for walking, cycling, climbing and other outdoor activities.

The rich diversity of the scenery of this comparatively small area is very much related to the underlying geology. In the south, the 'White Peak' is textbook limestone country, whilst the North has an overlay of gritstone, which results in a very different landscape, often referred to as the 'Dark Peak'.

The 'White Peak' has shapely hills such as Parkhouse Hill and Thorpe Cloud but the dales are the greatest attraction for visitors. Beautiful narrow valleys cut through the comparatively soft limestone by rivers such as the Dove, the Manifold and the Lathkill. The extensive areas of high plateaux, which separate these valleys, provide sharp contrast. Sparse and windswept, these areas support typical upland agriculture, the fields defined by endless miles of stonewalling. Also contrasting, is the landscape of the western and eastern fringes of this limestone area. In the west, from Waterhouses in the south to Lyme Park in the north, gritstone-based moorland constitutes a wide belt, which includes well-defined hills such as Shutlingsloe and great outcrops of rock, most notably the ridge of the Staffordshire Roaches. To the east, the series of gritstone 'edges' which form an almost continuous rim to the valley of the River Derwent are the outstanding feature. Within the limestone area are two 'islands' where the gritstone capping has endured; at Harthill Moor and Stanton Moor the vegetation and the visible evidence in the stone quarries are sure indicators of the differing geology.

The 'Dark Peak' of the north could hardly be more different. A huge area of land is significantly higher than the 'White Peak', a wild, wet, wilderness of moor – Kinder, Bleaklow and Black Hill – all capped by black peat, gouged into hags and groughs, supporting very scant life. Cotton grass provides just a little relief from the stark gloom of this forbidding landscape. Curiously enough, at 636m (2088ft), the highest point on Kinder is the actual 'peak', which gives the district its name. It would be hard to imagine anything less like a real peak.

Human occupation came early to the southern part of the district. The stone circles, burial chambers and human remains in caves all provide evidence of activity from 4000 years ago or more. Although now virtually deserted, the northern 'Dark Peak' area was formerly forested, with occupation initially by Mesolithic hunter/gatherers, before the transition to Neolithic farming brought about the progressive clearance of the oak, elm and lime woodland, resulting in what we see today.

Several of the dales have a good variety of broad-leaved trees, in some cases including the remains of ancient woodland. Nature conservation reserves have been established in many places. Modern plantations, such as those by the reservoirs in the upper part of the Derwent Valley, are extensive but hardly compensate for the loss of so much of the original woodland. The copses and shelter-belts of the limestone plateaux areas do soften that rather harsh landscape.

From the 14th century, great landowners have developed substantial estates in the more favoured places, with considerable effect on the landscape. Villages have been moved, deer parks created, and swathes of woodland form a backdrop to mansions such as Chatsworth and Haddon Hall. In the former case there is generous access available to walkers over a large part of the estate.

In 1951, Britain's first National Park was created, including the great majority of the Peak District, giving much-needed extra protection to a very vulnerable area. More than other National Parks, the district has suffered for many years from the operations of extractive industries on a very large scale, creating huge waste lands, particularly to the south and the east of Buxton which, for obvious reasons, have been excluded from the Park. Centuries of mining for lead and other minerals did vastly less damage to the landscape than the more recent quarrying, hacking away at the very substance of the countryside. Lesser areas of industrial activity are included in the Park, controlled as much as possible by the Park Authority. The cement works at Hope create a particularly unfortunate blot on the landscape.

Happily, these blemishes appear to have done little to diminish the attraction of the Peak District for walkers; indeed, the track along the lower part of the River Dove is claimed to be the most walked footpath in Britain.

In such a sensitive area, efforts have been made to minimise the adverse effects of the motor car, largely by encouraging motorists to leave their vehicles and to use public transport. The Goyt Valley scheme was a very early attempt to establish 'park and ride', and country bus services remain above average. Inducements such as 'Day Rover' tickets and special services such as the 'Peak Bus' network on Sundays and Bank Holiday Mondays also contribute to lessening the impact of the motor car. Up-to-date timetables are available from Tourist Information Centres. The Manchester to Sheffield railway service, calling at Chinley, Edale, Hope, Hathersage and Grindleford has long played a part in carrying walkers to and from the adjacent countryside.

With the obvious exception of the high, remote, moors in the north, the twenty-eight suggested routes in this book give a fair sample of the variety of landscape which makes up this alluring area.

1. Redmires Reservoirs and Rud Hill

Distance: 6.75km (4¼ miles)

Total ascent: 100m (328ft)

Start/car parking: Choice of parking areas along the reservoir access road. Recommended is an area under the trees, with picnic tables, grid reference 256857.

Refreshments: Take a picnic.

Map: Ordnance Survey Explorer OL 1, The Peak District, Dark Peak area, 1:25,000.

About the Walk

This is a walk circling the three linked reservoirs at Redmires, just a little off the beaten track, but very much on the Sheffield edge of the Peak District. Use is made of a well-waymarked permissive path over the high ground (Rud Hill) to the south of the reservoirs, coupled with the quiet cul-de-sac road along the northern and western edges of the water. A permissive path through the works area, with its woodland nature reserve, adds variety. The ascent to the moorland of Rud Hill is quite long but the gradients are gentle.

There are good, long views from parts of the route, notably over the western suburbs of Sheffield, particularly Fulwood.

The Walk

Leave the car park, turning right, along the access road by the top edge of the upper reservoir.

1. At the far end of the road bear right, up the unsurfaced 'by-way' road for 40m. Turn left along a narrow footpath through heather and bilberry, with a 'permissive path' sign. At a fork in a few metres go left, reaching a ladder stile in a further 40m. Continue through the bracken, crossing a tiny stream in its valley. Cross a bigger stream and rise to pass a lone rowan tree. Although a little overgrown in parts the path is not difficult to follow as it rises steadily.

2. Pass a waymark on a post and a large stone engraved 'SWW'.

Redmires Reservoir

There are more waymarks on posts, a few boulders and two trees on the skyline to the right as height is gained and the views become more extensive. At an area of boggy ground keep to the right; there is a waymark on a post on the far side. After more waymarked posts, rise towards a ladder stile in view ahead.

3. Go over the stile and head for another ladder stile, in the angle of stone walls, with first time views over the countryside to the right and the western part of Sheffield, ahead. Continue along the right edge of grazing land, with a wall on the right. Go downhill to a gate, with a waymark on an adjacent post. Follow the broad track ahead to the public road (Fulwood Lane).

4. Join the road at a gate/ladder stile. Turn left to walk by the roadside as far as Knoll Top Farm, passing Fulwood Head Farm on the way. Opposite Knoll Top Farm turn left at a gate/stile with 'public footpath' sign to follow a roadway into a former quarry. In less than 100m turn right at a signpost. In a further 200m turn

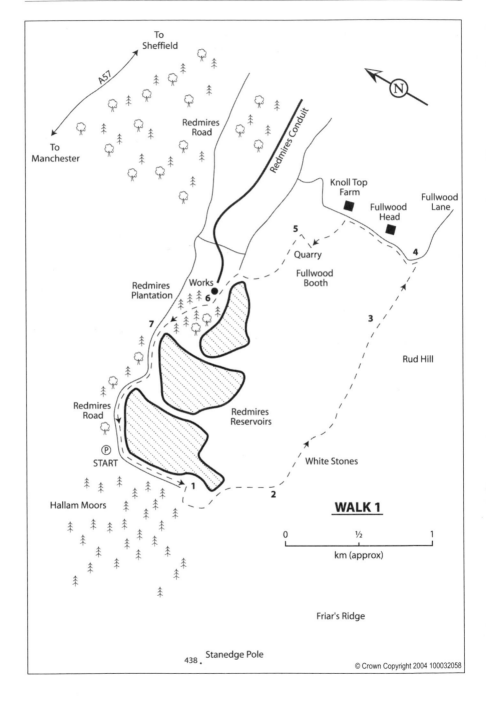

To
Sheffield

A57

To
Manchester

Redmires
Road

N

Redmires Conduit

Knoll Top
Farm

Fullwood
Head

Fullwood
Lane

5

Quarry

Fullwood
Booth

4

Redmires
Plantation

Works

6

3

Rud Hill

7

Redmires
Reservoirs

Redmires
Road

White Stones

P
START

1

2

WALK 1

Hallam Moors

0   ½   1

km (approx)

Friar's Ridge

438.   Stanedge Pole

right again, up a little bank. Cross the grass at the top for 70m to a waymarked 'City of Sheffield' stile.

5. Turn left along a grass lane. Ignore gates right and left, carrying on as the lane becomes a footpath, descending quite steeply towards the bottom end of the lowest reservoir. At the bottom bear left following a 'keep to the path' sign, below the dam of Lower Redmires Reservoir. A track between wall and fence now descends by the edge of a plantation. Cross over a rushing watercourse to reach the 'works' area. Turn right along a road (old 'footpath' sign).

6. Turn left at a road junction in 100m ('footpath' sign), approaching the gateway leading to a large building in a further 100m. Turn right ('footpath' sign) between fences, soon entering woodland, rising gently along a good path. Go over a major water conduit and an old stone stile to join the reservoir access the road.

7. Turn left to walk along the roadside back to the parking area in about three-quarters of a mile.

2. Edale

Distance: 6.25km (4 miles)

Total ascent: 125m (410ft)

Start/car parking: Large pay and display car park with public conveniences close to Edale railway station, grid reference 125854. There are railway services to and from Manchester and Sheffield and many intermediate stations. The Chapel-en-le-Frith to Castleton bus service (no. 200) calls at Edale.

Refreshments: Cafés at Edale station and Edale hamlet. Nags Head inn at Edale hamlet.

Map: As walk 1.

About the Walk

Edale and its valley has long been a favourite gathering place for walkers, even before the creation of the Pennine Way gave additional prestige as the starting or, more unusually, the finishing place for that first of the great long distance walks. It covers 250 miles or so of gruelling plod over high Pennine territory.

Edale is also significant as the division between the 'white peak' limestone country and the 'dark peak' gritstone. The latter is epitomised by the great mass of Kinder to the north, forming a tough introduction to much of what can be expected by the intrepid walkers setting off for the Scottish border. At 636m (2088ft.) the highest point in the National Park, Kinder is in fact the 'Peak' of the Peak District although the top is nothing like a real peak.

To the south of the valley the long high ridge includes, from the east, the graceful shape of Lose Hill, a meeting point of tracks at Hollins Cross, then Mam Tor and Rushup Edge.

Human activity in the valley has fortunately been generally confined to farming with little of the mineral and other extractive industry, which has so disfigured much of the district. The clustered settlements, all small, are called 'Booths'.

The Manchester to Sheffield railway line, with a reasonable service to Edale station, has always played an important role in transporting walkers to and from this fine area. Happily, this role

Edale

continues, with bus services also making a public transport contribution.

Edale itself is a very small village, with church, school and inn marking it as the focal point of the valley.

This circuit provides typical Edale walking without climbing any of the surrounding hills. However, for a 'level' walk the total ascent, almost all occurring in the early stages, is quite considerable, but at reasonable gradients. The necessary effort is rewarded by the views from this higher part of the route.

The Walk

Start beside the public conveniences, then go down a few steps to the road.

1. Turn right to walk along the roadside, under the railway line and passing the end of the station approach road. The road rises very gently, passing a visitor information centre/camping site, then Edale church, the Nags Head and the post office/general store.

2. Turn left at an 'Upper Booth' signpost. (Take care here – there is another signposted path to Barber Booth adjacent.) Go through a

kissing gate in a few metres to rise gently along a tiny valley with dry watercourse. At the top a gate leads into more open country-side.

3. In a further 40m go over a stile on the left, with a 'Pennine Way and Upper Booth' signpost. The path is now flagged for some distance, still rising across the flank of Broadlee Bank Tor, an outlying part of Kinder.

    The views across the valley to Lose Hill, Mam Tor and Rushup Edge are very fine. The surrounding area has extensive evidence of glacial moraines.

    There are several stiles as the clear path crosses the hillside before rising to a gate and a junction of routes. Keep left for 'Jacob's Ladder' and go over a stile before commencing the descent. There is one short, steep section before a gate is reached. There are several waymarks on posts and two gate/stiles before the track becomes a little lane. Follow this lane, soon joining another lane at Upper Booth hamlet.

4. Turn left, then in 20m, turn left again, through a gate with a 'foot-path' signpost. Pass a waymark on a post and follow the indi-cated line across a meadow. Cross a tiny stream on a slab bridge to reach a gate. Carry on in the same direction, through another gate, with a fence on the right. Cross another stream and go through two more gates, soon with the railway line close on the right. Turn right to cross the line on the bridge; the east portal of Cowburn tunnel, which takes the line for more than two miles under a great expanse of high moor before emerging in the Chinley area, is visible. Continue through a farm towards Barber Booth hamlet. Turn left at a fork in front of cottages, pass the trim Edale Methodist chapel and reach a road junction. Turn left to pass more attractive cottages in the main part of the hamlet.

5. In 100m go to the left at a gate signposted 'Grindsbrook Booth and Edale Station'. Rise gently along a broad unsurfaced track. Cross a bridge over the railway, turning right at a waymarked gate. At a waymarked gate there is a 'footpath to Edale' sign. There are more gates and waymarks on posts as the path crosses

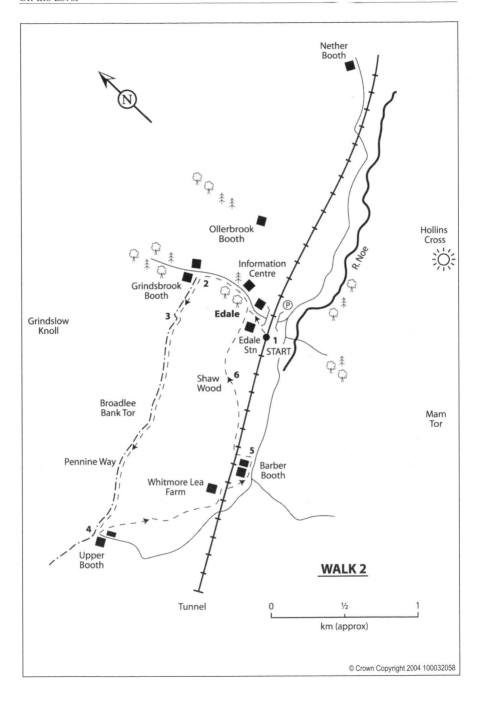

Nether
Booth

Hollins
Cross

R. Noe

Ollerbrook
Booth

Information
Centre

Edale

Grindsbrook
Booth

2

3

Grindslow
Knoll

Edale
Stn   **1**
START

Shaw   **6**
Wood

Broadlee
Bank Tor

Mam
Tor

Pennine Way

5

Whitmore Lea
Farm

Barber
Booth

4

Upper
Booth

WALK 2

Tunnel

0   ½   1

km (approx)

meadows, before rising gently to a signpost, a waymarked gate and a little bridge.

6. Cross an access drive to a waymarked gate on the far side, signposted 'Edale Station and Car Park', followed by a squeezer stile and a wide grass track along the edge of a meadow, heading for dwellings to the south of the village centre. After a gate/stile go across the front of cottages to a gate giving access to the public road. Rejoin the outward route, turning right to return to the car park.

3. Castleton

Distance: (Basic circuit) 4km (2½ miles). Including Castleton: 5.5km (3½ miles).

Total ascent: 120m (394ft). Including Castleton: 130m (427ft)

Start/car parking: Pay and display car park by the Speedwell Cavern entrance, half a mile west of Castleton, at the foot of the Winnatts Pass, grid reference 140828. Alternatively there are extensive roadside designated parking spaces on the adjacent former Mam Tor road, free except at weekends and Bank Holidays. Despite the awkward road access from the west, several bus services, including summer weekend and Bank Holiday special buses, reach Castleton. The widely available 'Hope Valley Leisure and Travel Guide' includes the relevant timetables.

Refreshments: None on the basic circuit. Wide choice in Castleton.

Map: As for walk 1.

About the Walk

In this circuit most of the ascent occurs early, with the steady rise to the old road near the Odin Mine followed by the road towards the foot of Mam Tor. Gradients are reasonable. Thereafter there is minor undulation, with a gentle rise back to the car park. If Castleton is included, the return to the car park involves a half mile of steady roadside ascent.

Underfoot, footpaths, lanes and a section of the former Mam Tor road are almost all good, with plenty of waymarking.

Backgroud

With good reason, Castleton is one of the most popular centres in the Peak District, an attractive and compact town sitting at the foot of the great scarp crowned by the ruins of Peveril Castle, built by King Henry II in 1176. Although the parish church was much restored in 1837, a Norman arch and box pews are still evident. Present day attractions include a small local history museum, a tourist information centre and no less than four sets of caverns open to the public. Shops, inns and cafés are plentiful. Surprisingly generous bus services include routes direct to Sheffield.

The surrounding area, close to the northern limestone (White

Peak)/gritstone (Dark Peak) divide, has been described as an open-air geology classroom, although much of the evidence is some way underground. A great deal of lead and some silver were mined locally for centuries, but the main mineral has for some time been the beautiful 'Blue John', found predominantly in the mine of the same name. Blue John is obtainable in the form of ornaments in several Castleton gift shops. The former Odin Mine (not open to visitors) is one of the oldest in the district, its vast workings explained by an information board on the line of this walk.

The Walk

From the car park walk to the former Mam Tor road, at the opposite end of the car park to the motor car entrance. Cross the road and turn right.

1. In 100m turn left along a surfaced lane with a 'Derbyshire Soaring Club' sign. At a junction in 100m go left to follow an unsurfaced lane.

    The views include the cleft of Winnatts Pass, the Treak Cliff Cavern buildings and the great 'shivering mountain' – Mam Tor. Win Hill, with its crowning 'pimple' is visible to the right.

    Reach Knowlegate Farm, with an old millstone in the yard. Turn left at a 'Mam Tor' signpost; go through a little gate and up steps to a stile at the top and a path rising through the bracken at a steady gradient, soon reaching a stile, with Mam Tor impressive ahead. Much of the ground here is obviously disturbed by previous mining activity, including the (protected) top of an old shaft a few metres to the right of the path. Continue under trees; pass a tiny spring then the striking monument of a mounted former grinding stone before rising to join the old road through a gate.

2. Turn right.

    Across the road is the entrance to the former Odin Mine, now owned by the National Trust. There is an excellent information board.

    Continue gently uphill, along the road.

    You soon pass a board explaining why, in an age of rocket science technology, the Highway Authority have had to abandon a major 'A'

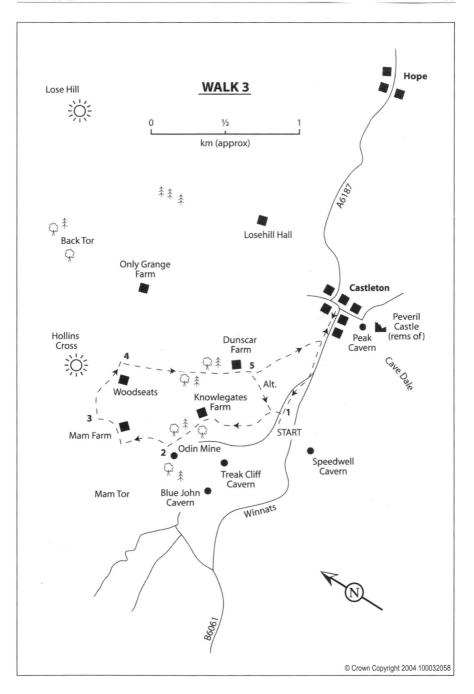

road, leaving Castleton without a good route to and from the west. Presumably, the Celts who built a village on top of Mam Tor 3000 years ago, were unaware of the underlying problems. Patching of the tarmac along the road is very evident, as is the fate of part of the road surface, below to the right.

3. As the road bends sharply to the left, terminating at a gate, turn right, downhill, along a signposted unsurfaced roadway to the National Trust Mam Farm. Go left, round the back of the farm, descending gently on a roadway. Rise to pass across the front of two houses, bearing right at the second, Tor House (signpost and waymark) to a gate. In 10m go through a waymarked gate then straight ahead across a wide field, the path not clear on the ground. There is a sleeper bridge over boggy ground then a waymark on a post. Keep up to the left to reach a little gate through a wall, then a stile. The path is now rather rough, staying fairly close to a fence on the right, passing well above Woodseats Farm before angling down to join the farm access roadway at a signposted stile.

4. Cross the roadway to a waymarked stile, opposite, to descend gently over grazed grass, keeping close to the stream/ditch on the right. After another stile continue the same line, facing Castleton, backed by Peveril Castle ruin on the scarp and the great gash of Peak Cavern. More waymarked stiles are passed, heading towards trees, the stream on the right now having a wooded valley, rich in willows. After a waymark on a post reach double gates/stiles and a signpost. Follow 'Castleton via Dirty Lane' to the left, with a fence and woodland on the left. Head for a waymark on a post, avoiding Dunscar Farm to the left. Go through a waymarked gate and diagonally across a small field to another signposted and waymarked gate/stile. Join a surfaced roadway, turning right to cross a stream on a bridge, reaching a junction in 25m.

5. **For the extension of the walk to Castleton** turn left here, signposted to 'Castleton via the Flats' Go over two stiles and along the edge of a meadow, with fence and stream on left. Go through a squeezer stile in a wall and follow a well-used track, crossing rough pasture to a gate and a narrow passageway to the public

Castleton and Mam Tor

road. Turn left by the roadside to head for the centre of the village; the distance to the church is barely 400m. To return to the parking area walk back along the roadside for about half a mile.

For the basic circuit stay with the roadway at point 5, soon reaching a junction with the outward route. Return to the Mam Tor road and the car park or roadside space.

4. Hope and Castleton

Distance: 6.5km (4 miles)

Total ascent: 45m (148ft)

Start/car parking: Pay and display car park in Hope village, grid reference 171835. Various bus services, including numbers 65 and 66 to and from Sheffield and Chesterfield, call at Hope on the way to Castleton.

Refreshments: Inns and the Woodbine tea shop in Hope. Wide choice in Castleton.

Map: As for walk 1.

About the Walk

The outward part of this circuit follows an excellent path staying close to the bank of Peakshole Water, facing Peveril Castle and Mam Tor for much of the way. After visiting Castleton, the return uses footpaths just a little higher on the north side of the valley, with correspondingly wide views. (unfortunately including the cement works). Ascent is minimal, with no steep gradients and no difficulties underfoot.

Background

An important trading centre in medieval times, the church being mentioned in the Domesday Book, Hope has continued as a busy little centre with several small shops, inns and tea shops. The presence of the main valley road and its traffic ensures that the village is functional rather than pretty. The present church probably stands on the site of a former Saxon church; a large fragment of a cross in the churchyard is claimed to be more than 1000 years old. Inside, largely renewed in the 14th century, there is a good deal to see including 15th-century windows.

Castleton is briefly described in walk 2.

The Walk

Turn right from the car park, along the side of the main road.

1. Turn right by the side of the church, along Pindale Road, with the church on the left. Cross the bridge over Peakshole Water,

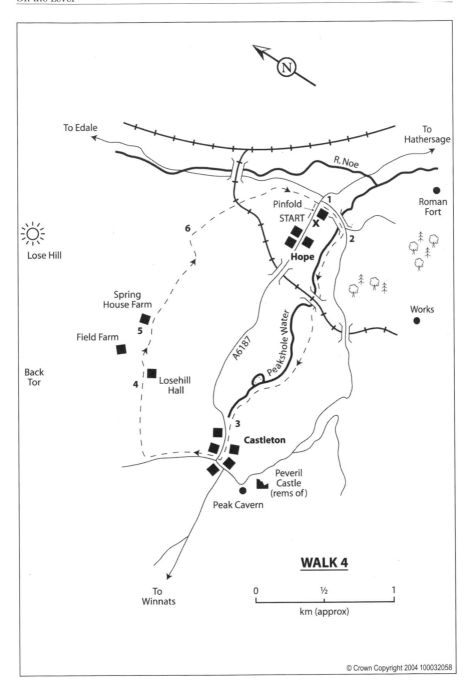

WALK 4

© Crown Copyright 2004 100032058

passing the renovated old pinfold (with an information board). Continue along the roadside as it rises past a junction with Eccles Lane.

2. 80m after that junction turn right, over a waymarked stile. There is a (damaged) sign of the historic Northern Footpaths Society. Follow the well-used path above the stream, noting Lose Hill and Win Hill in view to the right. After several stiles, the railway line, which serves the immense cement works, is crossed. Go over the stile on the far side of the line and continue over grass to a waymark on a post. There are more stiles and a gate as the path continues over meadows, eventually bearing right to stay beside the stream. Pass a small waterworks building and reservoir (on the far side of the stream) before going over a signposted stile. Carry on along a farm lane, passing farm buildings, then along a walled lane, to reach the main road

3. Turn left to walk along the roadside footpath to Castleton village. As the road bends sharply to the left near the village centre, turn right, along Back Street, leading to Mill Bridge. Cross the bridge over the stream, soon leaving the built-up area on a surfaced lane. Stay with the lane, rising very gently, to pass the Parish burial ground. Keep right as the lane forks; pass the Hollowford Centre (waymark on signpost). Keep right as the lane loses its surface, between walls, with an adventure play area and playing fields to the right. After a gate with cattle grid, turn right at once ('public footpath' sign) and keep to the right edge of a field to reach a stream with stepping stones and a waymarked gate. Keep to the left edge of the next meadow to a gate/squeezer stile giving access to an unsurfaced lane.

4. Go straight ahead along the lane. At a junction, with Field Farm to the left, bear right, through a gate. Win Hill is in view, ahead. Reach Spring House Farm and a junction of roadways. Turn left (signpost – 'Lose Hill and Hope'). Go through a gate in a few metres.

5. At a waymarked gate a few metres further turn right. The path is narrow but adequate; there are more gates. After going through a waymarked gate on the right, continue the same line to a

The ruin of Peveril Castle

waymarked kissing gate in 30m, then along the top edge of a field
to another waymarked gate, followed by a gate/squeezer
stile/bridge/steps. There are more gates and waymarks on posts
and another mini bridge as the path approaches Hope.

6. At a junction of paths turn right (signpost 'Hope' and another
historic footpath notice). Go through a waymarked gate, pass
another 'footpath' sign and go over another stile, with the village
in view ahead. Go through another gate, pass a house, then
another squeezer stile/little gate before crossing the cement
works railway line on a footbridge (for 20 persons only!). Go over
a stile, cross a meadow, then go through two more gates, continuing gently downhill towards Hope. There are more gates and a
four-way signpost. Follow 'Hope' to reach a residential avenue at
a gate/squeezer stile. Go across the avenue and then along the
avenue opposite (small school on left). Follow a passage between
houses, through a kissing gate, cross a small field to a kissing
gate, steps and the main road, almost opposite the Woodruff
Arms Hotel. Turn right to return to the car park.

5. Abney

Distance: 5km (3 miles)

Total ascent: 145m (476ft)

Start/car parking: By the roadside in or close to Abney hamlet, grid reference 199799. Abney is reached only by minor roads, from either Great Hucklow or Hathersage.

Refreshments: None

Map: Ordnance Survey Explorer (formerly Outdoor Leisure) OL24, The Peak District, White Peak area, 1:25,000.

About the Walk

This walk is a circuit around the modest green hill, Abney Low (in the Peak District, 'Low' = high). Obviously the chosen route reduces ascent to the minimum but there is still a fair amount, the longest rise being from Stoke Ford back to Abney, none of it being really steep, however. Apart from one short section somewhat overgrown with bracken, all paths are good.

Traditional farm buildings at Abney

Background

The countryside is very attractive, much of the route being along the fine wooded valleys of Bretton Clough and Abney Clough. Abney itself is an unremarkable farming hamlet, well off the beaten track.

The Walk

From the centre of Abney hamlet walk along the road towards Gt. Hucklow, passing a farm on the left. Continue downhill for a further 100m.

1. Turn left at a gate, signposted 'public footpath, Nether Bretton', to descend steeply on a little path, cross the stream at the bottom and ascend the other side, reaching a gate after a few steps. Continue along a narrow path on the side of a tributary valley before crossing a farm track and rising to a waymarked gate.

    Abney Low is in view to the left. The farmstead here is at the site of a round barrow (burial site) once surrounded by a stone circle

    Cross a meadow diagonally to a gate/stile in the far left corner, to the left of Cockey Farm. ('public footpath' signpost). Keep the wall on the left to pass to the left of the farm. There is a waymark on a post and another footpath sign. Carry on along the farm access drive.

    In view ahead, across the valley, are Bretton Moor and Broad Low.

2. Turn right, diagonally, at a footpath sign 100m after passing the farm. The path is not visible on the ground; head for another similar sign in 80m, followed by a stile over a wall.

    Away to the right is the high ground of Abney Moor, home of a gliding club.

    Keep to the left edge of the next meadow, passing a gate/squeezer stile to head downhill to Bretton Clough. After another stile the narrow path goes down the valley side, through the bracken at a reasonable gradient. At the bottom are steps and a plank bridge over a stream. After a stile, another plank bridge crosses Bretton Brook. Continue up the far side of the valley; steep for only a short distance.

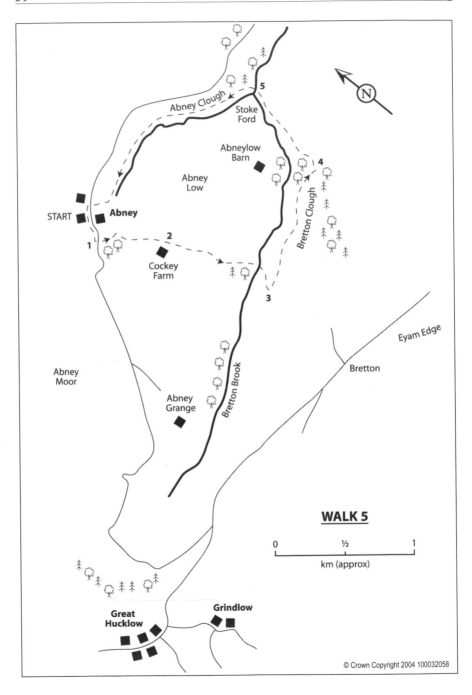

WALK 5

0   ½   1

km (approx)

© Crown Copyright 2004 100032058

3. A waymark on a post in less than 200m indicates straight on, up the hill. Ignore this and turn left along a narrow path. Cross a tiny stream, go over a broken wall and pass to the right of a mini knoll; there is a ruined building 40m to the left. Go over another broken wall and then bear well to the right of the trees ahead, the path leading into bracken before bearing left to resume the previous line. The path is a little overgrown but not difficult to follow, soon above a stone retaining wall on the left. Reach another old stone wall and then a junction of paths.

4. Go left, downhill, to a tiny stream and a stile. Continue along the side of Bretton Clough, now on a well-used track, up and down a little, with long views over the Abney Low countryside. Go left at a fork, through a broken stone wall and slightly downhill, with a ruined building above to the right. Go down more steeply over grass to reach woodland and a stile. Another path joins from the right as the track descends to Stoke Ford, at the junction of Abney and Bretton Cloughs, and a meeting place of several paths with a 'Peak District and Northern Counties Footpath Preservation Society' board of 1939.

5. Cross the bridge, then a stile, then another bridge and go left at a fork in 20m, 'footpath to Abney'. Rise through the woods of Abney Clough on a fine path, initially a little steep, but soon easing. Go through a gate, then pass two very old former gate posts before bearing right, up to a gateway and a little lane rising to join the public road in Abney.

6. Eyam and Foolow

Distance: 8km (5 miles) including a stroll around both villages

Total ascent: 105m (345ft)

Start/car parking: Roadside lay-by almost a quarter of a mile to the south of Foolow village, grid reference 192766 (or spaces in the village). Both Eyam and Foolow have bus services, including the 65/66 services linking Sheffield and Chesterfield with Buxton.

Refreshments: Tea shops and inns at Eyam. Bulls Head Inn at Foolow.

Map: 'White Peak' as for walk 5.

About the Walk

The outward route crosses upland agricultural country, with stiles in profusion and some gates, before descending into Eyam. The return is along a continuous lane, mainly unsurfaced, rising for some distance from Eyam. There are no problems underfoot although on the outward route the path is not always clear on the ground.

Background

The suffering of the population of Eyam during the 17th-century outbreak of bubonic plague has brought enduring fame to the village. Infection was brought to Eyam in a box of clothes sent from London to a tailor lodging in the village. The disease spread rapidly, with a very high fatality rate. Quite remarkably, led by the Rector, William Mompesson and his predecessor, Thomas Stanley, the villagers voluntarily isolated themselves from any contact with the outside world, thereby preventing spread of infection beyond the village boundary. Between 1665 and 1666, 259 of the population of about 350 died, including Mompesson's wife, Catherine.

Eyam still has many sad memorials of this great sacrifice, including the cottage where the outbreak started. On the fringe of the village are several sets of family graves and 'Cucklet Delf', to the south, where church services were held in the open to avoid increasing the risk of infection by congregating inside the church. Messages and goods from people outside the village were left at Mompesson's

The Rookery café and craft shop, Main Road, Eyam

Well, about half a mile along the minor road to the north. Washed coins were placed by the well in payment.

The church of St Lawrence has an 8th-century Celtic cross; the present church, believed to be the third structure on the site, largely dates from about 1350. Mompesson's carved oak chair, rescued from a Liverpool antique dealer, has been preserved in the church.

Eyam Hall has been the home of the Wright family for more than 300 years. A 17th-century manor house, it is open to the public from Easter to the end of August, on three days each week. Adjacent is a craft centre, open daily, other than Mondays, throughout the year.

A small local museum, situated close to the car park, has a full description of the plague among its collection.

After the plague, Eyam became prosperous as an industrial settle-ment, with lead mining, and the manufacture of cotton, silk and shoes all contributing at different times. Hall Hill troughs, which helped to provide the public water supply, can still be seen.

By contrast with Eyam, the tiny village of Foolow seems to have had an uneventful history. With its green, duck pond, a 14th-century cross and inn, it is certainly very attractive.

The Walk

From the lay-by, head along the roadside towards Foolow village, passing Ivy House Farm.

1. Just after the highway speed restriction sign, 150m before the village centre road junction, turn right over a stile ('public foot-path' signpost). Cross the parking area of a house to another stile in 25m, then another in 40m. Cross two fields diagonally, each with a stile. There are further signposts. Cross a rough field, heading for a signposted squeezer stile, passing a ruined small building. Keep to the right edge of the next three fields, separated by more stiles before descending via a few steps, into tiny Linen Dale.

2. Go through a signposted ('Eyam') gate and up the far side of the dale, now following a worn track. There are more stiles, then the right edge of a very rough meadow.

   The views to the left are of Eyam Edge, with the buildings of the Black Hole lead mine.

   After a gate/squeezer stile, go across a little lane and through five more stiles, continuing with a wall on the right and a little patch of woodland on the left. Eyam comes into view ahead as the path descends with a wall on the right. Go through one more stile before reaching a gate, then a stile and a passage between gardens, with steps.

3. Cross a surfaced lane, then a little field, then another surfaced lane. Continue along a footpath between gardens, still descending gently. Cross a residential avenue and continue between houses, then along another residential avenue, New Close.

4. Join the Eyam village street opposite the Eyam Craft Centre. (Turn right if you wish to access the main part of the village.)

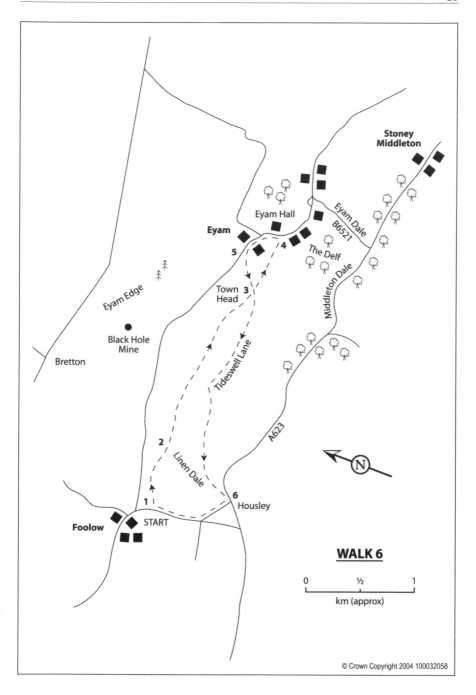

Stoney
Middleton

Eyam Hall

Eyam

Eyam Dale
B6521

5

4

The Delf

Town
Head

3

Middleton Dale

Eyam Edge

Black Hole
Mine

Tideswell Lane

Bretton

2

A623

N

Linen Dale

1

6

Housley

Foolow

START

WALK 6

0   ½   1

km (approx)

Turn left to continue the circuit, heading towards Townhead, passing some shops, a tea room/takeaway, the car park entrance and public conveniences. The museum is also close to the car park. Reach a junction with Tideswell Lane on the left.

5. Commence the return section by turning left here to rise steadily up the lane. Pass the junction with Windmill Lane and carry on rising, passing point 3 of the outward route. The lane loses its surface after the last house is passed. Ignore any turnings to right or left as the lane crosses the high ground, generally between stone walls but with views to both left and right.

    To the left, Middleton Moor is the high ground beyond the valley, which contains Stony Middleton village.

    Descend fairly steeply into Linen Dale, then go up the far side to join the minor public road close to the main A623 road.

6. Turn right to return to the parking lay-by (or Foolow village).

7. Grindleford, Hathersage and Bamford

Distance: (Bamford) 8 km (5 miles) (Hathersage) 4 km (2½ miles)

Total ascent: (Bamford) 40m (131ft) (Hathersage) 30m (98ft)

Start/car parking: Bamford railway station, grid reference 208825 or Hathersage railway station, grid reference 233810 (alternatively, travel by train!).

Refreshments: Plough Inn, near Hathersage (see below). Café at Grindleford station.

Map: Part 'White Peak', as walk 5, part 'Dark Peak' as walk 1.

About the Walk

After a downhill start, this walk is a virtually level stroll along the valley of the River Derwent, with longer or shorter options, using the train **from** Bamford or Hathersage **to** Grindleford station, then walking back to the starting place. Obviously, a reverse arrangement, initially driving to Grindleford, walking, then returning on the train, is also possible. The three stations are all served by the stopping trains of the Manchester to Sheffield service, at hourly or two-hourly intervals, depending on the time of the day.

Most of the route is along footpaths designated as the 'Derwent Valley Heritage Way', with a fine mixture of woodland and more open areas, easy to follow and with no difficult sections. Close to the start, there is a relatively steep descent for a few metres in Coppice Wood. Roadside walking is minimal.

Background

Grindleford railway station is situated some distance from the village of the same name, attractively tucked under the wooded lower slopes of Froggatt Edge at Upper Padley, adjacent to the Longshaw Estate, in National Trust ownership. Close to the station is the west portal of the great Totley tunnel, second in length only to the Severn tunnel. The tunnel was opened to traffic in 1893, the last of the trans-Pennine railway links. The route of the walk passes Padley Mill, then Padley Chapel, which is the remaining part of the

The famous Grindleford station café with, left, exhortations to try the local water

NATURAL SPRING WATER

The climber, cyclist, runner to all come in and have a brew, but the day is long & not yet through, so take along some natural too; The water will quench the driest thirst to allow you one more burst You pinch the rock, grip your bike or dig in your set of spikes You reach your goal and struggled through. Could it be that special brew Sparkle or Still which ever you like You go upon your hike Set your sights at dizzy heights and let your spirit soar Grindleford Natural Spring Water holds you to your chore

former Padley Hall of the 14th and 15th centuries, place of the arrest of two Roman Catholic priests in 1588. The priests were subsequently executed, in the gruesome fashion of the time, at Derby.

Hathersage is a substantial village, with inns, shops and other facilities, situated close to high moorland and the famous Stanage Edge. The church, of the 14th and 15th centuries, has a 14th-century tower and spire. Inside, there is much evidence of the Eyre family, locally prominent for many generations; other interesting features include the canopied sedilia (ceremonial seat), the piscina (basin set into the wall) and fine capitals surmounting the shafts of the columns. The alleged grave of Little John, close compatriot of Robin Hood, is in the churchyard. The village has strong associations with Charlotte Brontë.

The Walk

From the station platform turn right to walk to the adjacent station approach road.

1. Turn left to cross a bridge over Burbage Brook and reach Padley Mill. Continue along an unsurfaced roadway, rising a little after passing the mill. Pass semi-detached houses, the road now having a hard surface. Descend to pass Brunt's Barn. Pass Padley Chapel, now an 'ancient monument'. Reach a gate/cattle grid with a National Trust 'Longshaw Estate' board. Turn left in 40m through a waymarked kissing gate, cross the bridge over the railway line and follow a fine path descending gently towards the River Derwent. Pass a junction of paths, bearing right by a small cluster of trees. At a signposted gateway turn right, along the near side of the wall, the path now much less evident. Go through a gap in a wall and continue towards gateposts showing the way through the next wall.

2. Head for a kissing gate through the next wall, entering National Trust land at Coppice Wood (Longshaw Estate). Follow the clear path through the woodland, descending quite steeply for a short distance; where the path divides, either branch will suffice. At a junction in 100m turn right, now descending more gently.

3. Join a major track by the bank of the river; turn right, soon leaving Coppice Wood at a gate with a 'Derwent Valley Heritage Way' waymark. Continue over grazed grass, soon bearing a little to the right, away from the river, through a broken wall, reaching the large property 'Harper Leas' (sign). Pass a waymark on a post, then go through a signposted kissing gate to join a surfaced road, turning left, now by the side of the river again.

   Here there are sculpted stones and other apparently salvaged items, some of them forming an impromptu picnic area.

   Pass a post with waymarks, going straight on along the surfaced roadway. Reach a gate/cattle grid with waymarks on post, then another gate/cattle grid, reaching the public road by a squeezer stile.

4. This is the point of decision:

For Hathersage railway station, either turn right to walk by the roadside for a little more than a quarter of a mile before turning right again after crossing under the line **or** take the signposted footpath on the far side of the road, keeping to the right at a junction of paths, to avoid some of the roadside.

For the full walk to Bamford turn left, cross Leadmill Bridge over the river and turn right immediately at a 'Shatton' signpost. *Note that the Plough Inn is a very short distance round the next bend.* Pass a gate and a waymark on a post before reaching the gate giving access to Goose Nest Wood (Peak District National Park Authority). The path through the wood is narrow in places but not difficult. Leave the wood through a gate after crossing a footbridge over a stream. There are more gates and another footbridge, followed by a section of path close to the river, where erosion has made it necessary to step partially into the adjacent meadow. Nether Hall (farm – on the far side of the water) is passed.

The views include High Low, Offerton Moor and Shatton Moor to the left, with the more distant Mam Tor ahead.

Go through more gates before reaching a four-way signpost; to the right are stepping-stones across the river.

5. Follow 'Shatton', straight ahead. At a section of steep, high, river bank go up a flight of steps with a 'Shatton' signpost at the top, soon descending steeply to a gated plank bridge over a stream and a farm roadway. Continue by the riverside.

Bamford Edge and Lose Hill are to the right, Mam Tor is ahead.

Pass Kentney Barn and its sheepfold, go through gates and cross a gated bridge over a stream. The path passes under trees, a little up and down, to a footbridge over a stream.

6. Join a public road through/over a gate or stile. Shatton village, of no particular distinction, is to the left. Turn right, cross the road bridge over the river, reaching the A6187 at a road junction. Turn right to walk by the roadside past a garden centre. Cross the river

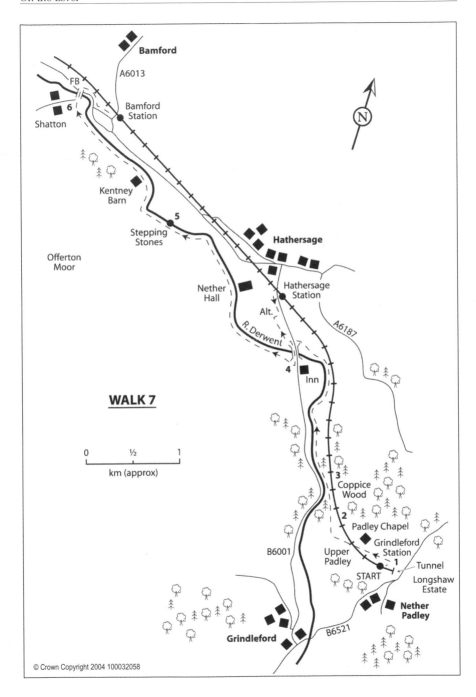

Bamford

A6013

FB

6

Shatton

Bamford
Station

Kentney
Barn

Offerton
Moor

Stepping
Stones

5

Nether
Hall

Hathersage

Hathersage
Station

Alt.

R. Derwent

A6187

4

Inn

WALK 7

0   ½   1

km (approx)

Coppice
Wood

3

2

Padley Chapel

Grindleford
Station

B6001

Upper
Padley

1

Tunnel

START

Longshaw
Estate

**Nether
Padley**

Grindleford

B6521

N

© Crown Copyright 2004 100032058

again on a footbridge adjacent to the road bridge. At the far end of the bridge turn left along a residential roadway, rising gently to join the A6013 close to Bamford station. Cross the road, turning left, then right, down the steps, to the 'Sheffield' platform and a through a little gate to the car park.

8. Calver and Froggatt

Distance: 4km (2½ miles)

Total ascent: negligible.

Start/car parking: Space by the roadside close to the old Calver Bridge – a loop off the A623, grid reference 247745. There are more spaces along Dukes Drive (cross the river and turn left).

Refreshments: Bridge Inn by Calver Bridge. Café at Country Crafts, Calver Bridge.

Map: 'White Peak' as walk 5.

About the Walk

A very undemanding level stroll, using excellent paths, with generally good signposting, on each side of the River Derwent.

Background

Sitting below the long gritstone scarp of Froggatt Edge, the village of Froggatt is a rather scattered community by the side of the River Derwent. The best features are the 17th-century bridge and the 'new' bridge, both spanning the river.

The new bridge over the River Derwent near Froggatt

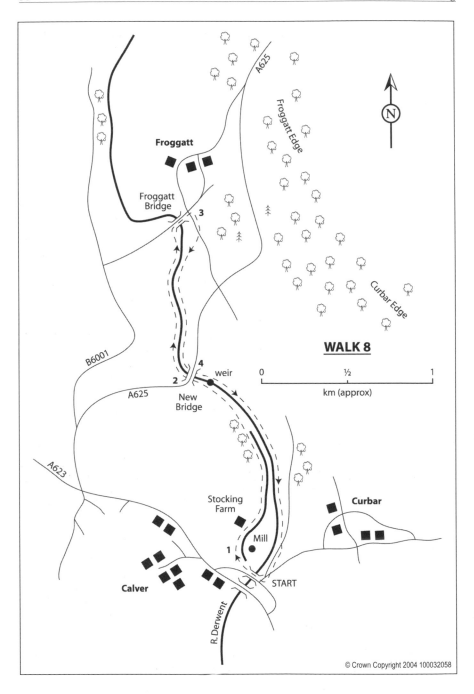

WALK 8

0   ½   1
km (approx)

Calver is a residential area, by-passed by the main A623 road, with old and new bridges across the river. Close to the bridge is a large former cotton mill, with associated waterways and a great weir a long way upstream of the mill. The mill has been converted for residential use.

The Walk

Set off along the lane signposted 'Calver Mill, also 'public footpath, New Bridge and Froggatt'.

1. Pass the entrance to Calver Mill, on the right in 100m. Continue along the surfaced drive to Stocking Farm. At the farm, with its small caravan site, note the former bell housing and old buildings. Bear right, then left to a waymarked (Derwent Valley Heritage Way) gate. Continue across a meadow on a well-worn path, with Froggatt Edge in view. Pass a waymark on a post before reaching the side of the substantial leat (known as the Goit) which conducted water to the mill. Follow the broad path by the side of the leat, under trees; the main course of the River Derwent is 50m to the right. Pass a vehicular barrier and rise past two bungalows to join a public road beside New Bridge.

2. Cross the road to a signpost opposite and carry on along the riverside path. For some distance the river is, in effect, a large millpond. Cross a stream on a footbridge; to the left is a swampy area, rich in scrubby willow. Go through a kissing gate, pass a waymark on a stump, go through a squeezer stile and approach Froggatt Bridge (this side has the clearest view of the structure). Go over a waymarked stile to join a public road. Turn right and cross the bridge.

3. Turn right at the far end of the bridge (signpost 'Sheffield'). In 100m turn right, over a stile (no signpost or waymark) to follow a clear path through the trees, close to the river bank, soon crossing a bridge over a dry stream bed. The path is narrow in places and a little overgrown. Reach New Bridge and go up a short flight of steps to the public road.

4. Go straight across the road to a signpost and take a broader path, soon reaching one end of the great weir, which ensured adequate

water supplies for Calver Mill. Rise gently to a tiny footbridge over a dry streambed and go through a little gate, then another, signposted, gate, to join a minor road, Dukes Drive. Turn right, to walk by the roadside, with Calver Mill and comparatively new additions visible across the river. Reach a road junction opposite the Bridge Inn. Turn right to cross the river on a footbridge beside the old road bridge and return to the parking area.

9. Curbar Gap, White Edge and Froggatt Edge

Distance: 9½km (6 miles)

Total ascent: 160m (525ft)

Start/car parking: Pay and display car park at Curbar Gap, grid reference 262747. Accessed by the minor road, which climbs up the side of the Derwent Valley, through Curbar village, from the A623 by the Bridge Inn at Calver.

Refreshments: Grouse Inn.

Map: 'White Peak' as walk 5.

About the Walk

This circuit is very much at the 'tough' end of level walking, with a considerable amount of ascent. The total is, however, split between several different sections, notably close to the start and close to the finish, over a comparatively long distance and there are no really steep gradients. It provides a great opportunity for 'level' walkers to tramp over comparatively high moorland, enjoying the very long views consistent with heights of more than 300m (985ft).

The outward route is along White Edge, a very modest line of raised ground, with the return along the top of Froggatt Edge, a much more spectacular scarp overlooking the valley of the River Derwent. For such rough country, the paths are surprisingly good. About half a mile beside the A625.

Background

Froggatt Edge, beloved of rock climbers, is one of the finest of the gritstone scarps of the eastern part of the Peak District. The path along the top has superb views over a long section of the valley of the River Derwent, including several villages. Behind Froggatt Edge a small prehistoric stone circle is not too difficult to find.

White Edge, although higher, is less spectacular but does have views over the moorland to the east.

Froggatt Edge

The Walk

Leave the car park through a gate at the side of the vehicular entrance, passing an 'Eastern Moors Estate' notice board. Proceed along a wide, rough, track.

1. Go straight on at a fork in 100m – enclosed fields on the slope ahead show the efforts made to wrest a living from this unpromising land. Cross a tiny stream on a plank bridge and commence the first ascent by the side of a stone wall.

2. At the top, with signpost, turn left for 'Longshaw', rising more gently through the heather and bracken along the top of White Edge. There are occasional waymarks on posts; the track is always obvious. At a fork, bear right (waymark on post) to a trig point (365m, 1180ft). Continue walking – the edge becomes better defined, with the roughness softened by rowan and silver birch trees.

The relatively flat farming country of Stoke Flat is evident below and the Grouse Inn is also in view.

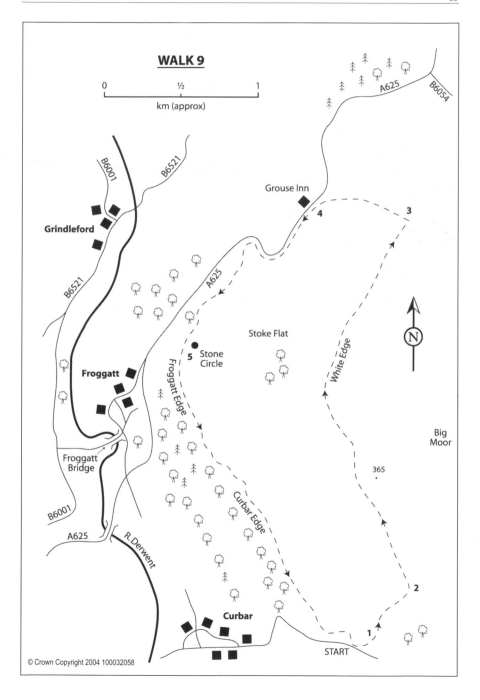

WALK 9

0 ½ 1
km (approx)

A625

B6054

B6001

B6521

Grouse Inn

4

3

Grindleford

B6521

A625

White Edge

N

Stoke Flat

5 Stone Circle

Froggatt Edge

Big Moor

Froggatt

365

Froggatt Bridge

Curbar Edge

B6001

A625

R. Derwent

2

Curbar

1

START

3. Reach an old stone wall at a signpost. Turn left for the 'Grouse Inn'. The track stays beside a broken stone wall, descending steeply into a wooded valley, for a short distance on rough ground. At a signposted junction go left for the 'Grouse Inn'. There may be some mud by a gate, then a path across a rough meadow, leading straight to the inn. Go through a gate to join the public road.

4. Turn left either to visit the inn or to continue the walk by the roadside, mainly on verge, for about half a mile. After a right-hand bend go left to a gate and a rising track with one of the 'Eastern Moors Estate' signs. Go over a stile beside a gate, still rising through silver birch woodland. Go through a gate. In about 200m, a short diversion along a minor track to the left reveals a little prehistoric stone circle, about 15m in diameter, largely obscured by bracken. Many of the stones are displaced or missing.

5. Continue along the top of Froggatt Edge, with fine rock scenery, extensive views including Calver and Curbar, and a steady ascent towards a prominent rock outcrop. At a fork, the easier route is round to the left, better underfoot than the more direct route. Descend towards the car park, go through a gate and bear left to return.

10. Baslow and Curbar

Distance: 6km (3¾ miles)

Total ascent: 175m (574ft)

Start/car parking: Pay and display car park close to the side of the main A619 in Baslow, grid reference 258721. However, finding a parking place on the residential road Eaton Hill, close to the junction with Bar Road, reduces the distance by a kilometre (two-thirds of a mile) and the total ascent by about 25m (82ft). Bus services to Baslow include the 213/214 Sheffield to Wirksworth, the 66 Chesterfield to Buxton, the 171 Chesterfield to Hartington and the Sundays/Bank Holidays 181 Sheffield to Hartington.

Refreshments: Inns and tea shop in Baslow, close to the car park.

Map: 'White Peak' as walk 5.

About the Walk

The ascent at the start of this walk, particularly from the Baslow car park, is considerable and the total is quite high for a 'level' book. However, the outward path high across the slopes below Baslow Edge, with its fine views over the Derwent valley, makes the effort worthwhile. The return route to Baslow is much closer to the valley bottom, along footpaths and a lane through agricultural land. Apart from the chance of some wet ground when approaching Curbar, there are no problems underfoot; the only roadside walking is a short length at Curbar and through the residential area of Baslow.

Background

The large village of Baslow, well-situated below the Derwent Valley gritstone edges and not far from Chatsworth Park, suffers from the effect of traffic on the busy A619. However, the quieter area by the old bridge has old houses and the parish church . Much of the latter is 14th century; inside is a great deal of modern carved oak.

The scattered dwellings of Curbar climb the hillside towards the Edge of the same name. The church is very much at the foot of the village, close to Calver Bridge and the River Derwent. A former pinfold (a pen used for confining strayed livestock) and a covered well can still be found in Curbar.

The Walk

From the car park cross the A619 by the pedestrian traffic lights and walk up Eaton Hill, opposite. As the road bears to the left, turn right to continue up Bar Road, which soon loses its hard surface.

1. As Bar Road bends to the right, turn left at a stile to take a footpath rising invitingly through the gorse. By the stile is a spring, marked as 'Lady Wall Well' on the OS map. Go through/over a gate/stile in 150m. The path continues to rise fairly gently. Go over a ladder stile, pass a 'footpath' sign and join a farm roadway in 50m.

    The extensive views on this part of the walk include much of the Derwent Valley, with Gorse Bank Farm, below, and Baslow Edge, above.

Gorse Bank Farm, Baslow

2. Turn right along the roadway, soon a lane with widely-spread walls, and obviously an old drove-way. As the way bends sharp right, go straight ahead with a wall close on the left ('footpath' sign on wall). Go over a stile by a locked gate, pass an 'Eastern Moors Estate' board, and continue across a hillside strewn with gritstone boulders. Go straight ahead at a cross-paths in 100m to

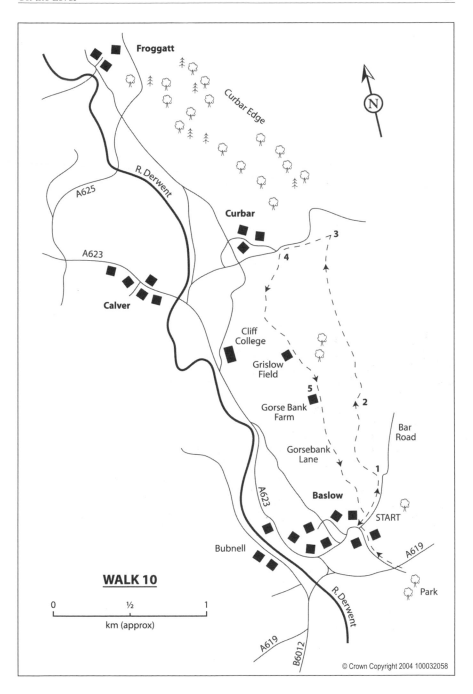

Froggatt

Curbar Edge

N

R. Derwent

A625

A623

Calver

Curbar

3

4

Cliff
College

Grislow
Field

5

Gorse Bank
Farm

Gorsebank
Lane

2

Bar
Road

1

Baslow

START

A619

Bubnell

Park

WALK 10

0   ½   1

km (approx)

A623

A619

B6012

R. Derwent

© Crown Copyright 2004 100032058

follow a well-used track through the bracken, with Calver village in view, below. At a fork, bear right, uphill. Approaching Curbar, the path becomes rather diffuse among boulders, bracken and some swampy ground. Head for a post with notice boards, by a gate through a stone wall. Go through the gate. Adjacent is a ' National Trust, Curbar Gap' sign. Go through a squeezer stile on the left.

3. Descend over grass towards Curbar village, going through a squeezer stile to join the public road. Turn left to walk down the road. Ignore the first footpath sign on the left.

4. Turn left at a 'public footpath to Baslow via Grove Bank Farm' sign and follow a surfaced lane.

   To the left is an odd building, not unlike a dovecote. However, it was used for short-term holding of prisoners who were awaiting transport to distant gaols.

   By the entrance to Lane Farm is a cattle grid and 'private' notice. Go through the little gate on the right to follow a walled path past the farm. Ignore a path to the right, staying with the clear path; go through/over a waymarked gate/stile before reaching a waymarked and signposted gate. Turn left here, pass a waymark on a post, then a waymarked gate, for a short, sharp ascent past Grislow Field (farm). Bear right at the top, go through a sign-posted gate in 30m then straight across a narrow field to a gate-way, followed by a squeezer stile in 40m. Rise gently to Gorse Bank Farm.

5. Go through a gate, to pass between the farm buildings then follow the surfaced lane back to a junction with Bar Road in Baslow. Turn right to return to the car park.

11. Chatsworth

Distance: 6½km (4 miles)

Total ascent: 145m (476ft)

Start/car parking: Main car park (pay) for visitors to Chatsworth House/gardens, grid reference 260703. The 213/214 Sheffield to Wirksworth bus service stops at Edensor Gates, for Chatsworth.

Refreshments: Large café/restaurant/bar complex adjacent to Chatsworth House. Also, kiosks for casual refreshments.

Map: 'White Peak' as for walk 5.

About the Walk

As with so many walks, the bulk of the ascent is at the start, a steady rise past the adventure playground, quite steep at first, along a surfaced roadway. Most of the outward route is on surfaced roadway, rising gently across the extensively wooded hillside above the House to a summit at Beeley Moor. After a good path descending the side of the moor, the bulk of the return route is along the idyllic grass footpath by the side of the River Derwent.

Chatsworth House

Background

Chatsworth House is among the stateliest of stately homes, a huge property of Elizabethan origins, much enlarged and altered between 1686 and 1707, then again in the 1820's. Still the home of the Duke and Duchess of Devonshire (Cavendish family), the house, a veritable treasure trove, is open to the public, together with its extensive and elaborate gardens. Both Capability Brown and Joseph Paxton were involved, the latter as head gardener for a long period. Paxton is, of course, better known as the designer of the celebrated Crystal Palace in London. Extensive glass houses at Chatsworth were forerunners of that monumental enterprise. An animal farm and adventure playground are of great attraction for children.

Surrounding the house and garden is the great expanse of Chatsworth Park, much of it laid out by Capability Brown. Most of this area, criss-crossed by tracks, is available to walkers.

The Walk

Go uphill from the car park, keeping to the left of the restaurant building, heading for the farmyard/adventure playground.

1. Pass a cattle grid and fork right in 40m at a 'Stand Wood' sign. The roadway rises quite steeply initially. Go round a sharp right bend, still rising.

    Ignore a track on the left. The vegetation is very rich, including many rhododendrons. Go straight on at a junction, soon among pine forest. After passing a red and mauve waymark, go round a left hairpin bend, with a very old yew tree apparently growing out of the rock. In 150m go round a right hairpin bend. Ignore any track to left or right.

2. About 100m after the bend, fork right along a grass track, soon reaching a little rocky point with views over the Derwent Valley. Join a rough surfaced track and carry on to a wall with a locked gate and a high ladder stile giving access to open moorland. Follow the rising path.

3. Turn right in 100m to take a waymarked path descending through the dense bracken. The path is quite steep initially and narrow in places. Go over a stile to cross a meadow and go over

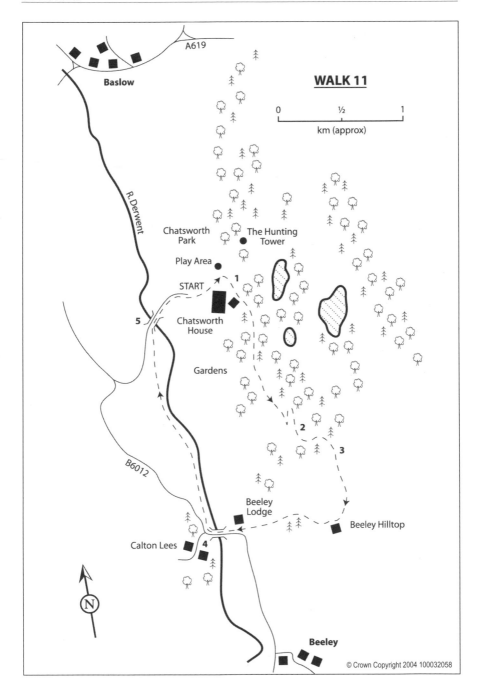

Baslow

A619

WALK 11

0   ½   1

km (approx)

R. Derwent

Chatsworth
Park

The Hunting
Tower

Play Area

START

1

5

Chatsworth
House

Gardens

2

3

B6012

Beeley
Lodge

Beeley Hilltop

Calton Lees

4

N

Beeley

© Crown Copyright 2004 100032058

another stile to join a lane close to farm buildings (Beeley Hill-top). Turn right, downhill, to walk past another part of the farm, then through woodland to reach Beeley Lodge. Join the public road, turning right to walk by the roadside, crossing the bridge over the River Derwent.

4. Immediately after the bridge turn right, through an old kissing gate, and follow the delightful grass path beside the river for a little more than 1 mile. Pass the ruin of the well-constructed old mill, two stepped weirs and several seats. There are fine specimens of trees, mainly oak and sycamores, and a good view of the House. Bear left at a fence and rise to join the Chatsworth access road.

5. Turn right to cross the bridge, then fork right along a pedestrian route, through a gate, to return to the car park.

12. Great and Little Longstone

Distance: (basic circuit) 6km (3¾ miles) (with extension to Monsal Head) 7 km (4¼ miles)

Total ascent: 62m (203ft) (with extension to Monsal Head) 92m (302ft)

Start/car parking: Roadside lay-by for 5 vehicles by the telephone box and old parish-pump in Little Longstone, grid reference 191718. If including Monsal Head, large pay and display car park, with public conveniences and views, by the side of the Monsal Head Hotel, grid reference 185715. Bus services 4 and 173 call at these villages.

Refreshments: Café at Monsal Head. Inns at Monsal Head, Little Longstone and Great Longstone.

Map: 'White Peak' as for walk 5

About the Walk

This circuit includes two interesting and pleasant villages and a section of the Monsal Trail, along the trackbed of the former Midland Railway. There are no serious ascents, just two short uphill sections. Some walking by the (quiet) roadside, including village streets. No problems underfoot.

Background

The substantial village of Great Longstone has a small green, with ancient cross, at one end of the village street. There are also shops and inns and a church dating in part from the 13th century. The 15th century roofs have fine moulded beams and carved bosses.

A short distance along the road to the west, Little Longstone has just one small inn and attractive cottages with pretty gardens.

Monsal Head is an outstanding viewpoint, perched high above the valley of the Wye. By the car park are an inn, a café and a picnic area.

The Walk

From a start at Little Longstone walk along the roadside towards Great Longstone. **From Monsal Head**, leave the car park, cross the main road, and walk by the side of the road opposite, as far as Little

Longstone. Pass the Packhorse Inn before reaching the parking lay-by.

The Packhorse Inn

1. In 60m, turn right to leave the road. There are two 'footpath' signposts. Go over the stile on the left, signposted 'public footpath, Great Longstone'. Rise up the meadow on the line indicated by the signpost, to a stile at the top. Go over another stile in 20m then diagonally across a meadow along the visible path. There are views to Longstone Edge to the left. Go through a waymarked squeezer stile at the far right corner. Cross the end of a little lane, then through a gate/squeezer stile, then another in 25m then along a path across the middle of a field to the edge of Great Longstone. Join a residential road via a signposted squeezer stile.

2. Turn left to walk to the main part of the village. At a road junction is a tiny green and the base of the old cross (the Crispin Inn is to the left). Turn right to walk along the village street, passing the White Lion Inn, butcher's shop, village store and the Croft Country House Hotel. Stay with the main road at a junction, leaving Great Longstone along the roadside footpath. At the next road junction turn left, uphill, along Mires Lane. Pass the house 'Arma Meadow' before reaching a more important road. Turn left for 40m, passing Buskey Cottage.

3. Turn right, through a signposted squeezer stile, then through another stile in 15m to continue along the right edge of a large meadow, with a wall on the right, to a waymarked gate/stile. The

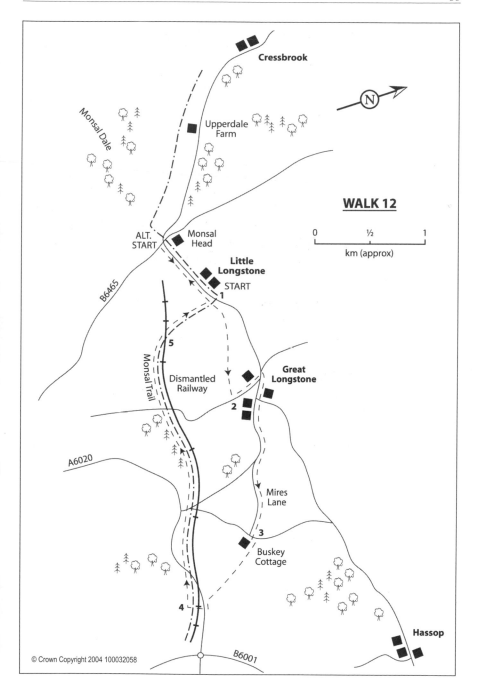

Cressbrook

Monsal Dale

Upperdale
Farm

N

WALK 12

ALT.
START

Monsal
Head

Little
Longstone
START
1

B6465

5

Monsal Trail

Dismantled
Railway

Great
Longstone

2

A6020

Mires
Lane

3
Buskey
Cottage

4

Hassop

© Crown Copyright 2004 100032058

B6001

0   ½   1
km (approx)

path across the next field is not well defined. Keep to almost the same line, descending gently to aim for a signposted gate/stile to the right of Toll Bar House. Cross the main road and turn left for 80m to a gate opposite Toll Bar House, with a 'public bridleway' signpost. Follow the track across a rough little field to a gate giving access to the former railway line – the Monsal Trail.

4. Turn right, along the Trail. Cross a bridge over a road, go under a bridge, cross another bridge over a road junction, go under another bridge, pass a seat, now with views to Longstone Edge and to the residential edge of Great Longstone. After passing under two more bridges, reach the platforms and converted buildings of the former Great Longstone station. Continue; the point at which the Monsal Trail leaves the railway line because of the approach to the tunnel under Monsal Head is not much further.

5. Turn right through a signposted stile to follow a well-worn track by a wall on the left, rising very gently to a little gate. Carry on to another gate and rejoin the outward route at the road in Little Longstone. Turn left to the parking place.

    To continue to Monsal Head (or return to the car park if used as a starting place) walk by the roadside for a further half mile, rising all the way.

13. Millers Dale

Distance: 5.25km (3¼ miles)

Total ascent: 25m (82ft)

Start/car parking: The former Millers Dale railway station, now a centre for the Monsal Trail, based on the old railway line, with information and public conveniences, grid reference 139733. Pay and display. Signposted along the Wormhill road from the main road in Millers Dale. Bus services 65 and 66, Buxton to Sheffield and Buxton to Chesterfield call at Millers Dale.

Refreshments: Anglers Rest Inn, Millers Dale

Map: 'White Peak' as for walk 5

About the Walk

The outward part of this circuit uses the Monsal Trail along the trackbed of the former railway line, as far as Litton Mill, with the return along the minor cul-de-sac road which serves the mill and its cottages. This road stays beside the River Wye. The only significant ascent is the return to the car park, either by the roadside or by the (preferred) return via the railway trackbed. The descent from the railway line at Litton Mill and the (optional) rise to the line on the return are both fairly steep and stony but without difficulty; otherwise the going is entirely easy.

Background

Millers Dale is, without doubt, scenically one of the finest parts of the valley of the River Wye. It is squeezed between the steep sides and rocky bluffs which forced the engineers of the Midland Railway to tunnel extensively and to construct viaducts and dig cuttings when building their enterprising line through this difficult territory. Linking Manchester (Central) with London (St Pancras) via Derby, the line was opened in 1867. John Ruskin was among those who denounced the ruination of a previous rural paradise. As a through route from Manchester to London the line could not compete with the rival London and North Western/Staffordshire Railway routes via Crewe or Stoke, but it did also serve several of the cities and towns of the East Midlands. Millers Dale station was a junction, with branch line trains for Buxton leaving from a bay platform. Closed in 1968, long sections of the line, designated as the 'Monsal Trail', now give pleasure to walkers and cyclists by providing easy access to lovely countryside.

Old machinery, Litton Mill

Engineering works, such as the double viaduct at Millers Dale and the fine structure below Monsal Head (not on the line of this walk), also add interest to the Trail. There are information boards at the old station.

The little church at Millers Dale hamlet was built in 1880.

The sizeable Litton Mill, with its adjacent cottages, is tucked away in the valley bottom at the end of a long very minor road. The mill is now converted into residential apartments.

The Walk

Pass through the gate by the end of the old station building to reach the former trackbed.

1. Turn left, crossing a bridge over the adjacent road, followed by the lower of the side-by-side viaducts, high over the deep, narrow, valley.

2. Footpaths leave the Trail on either side; Priestcliffe Nature Reserve is to the right. At the next junction, 'Ravenstor' is signposted to the left, with another nature reserve to the right. A more open section has views to Hammerton Hill on the left, followed by Litton Mill cutting, a Site of Special Scientific Interest managed by English Nature. Continue under a brick bridge

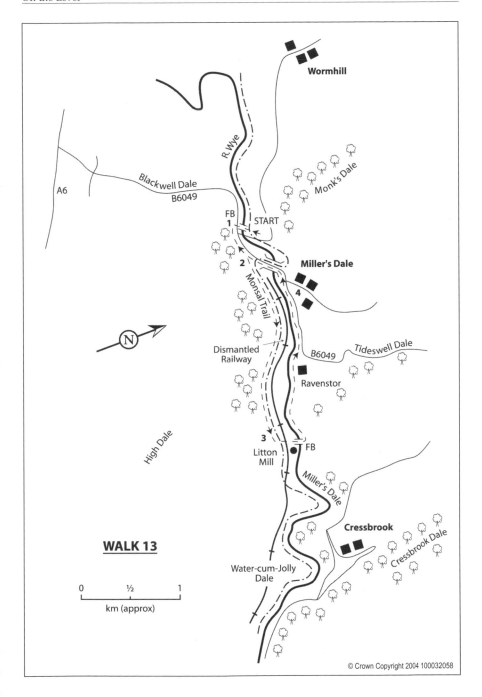

Wormhill

R.Wye

Monk's Dale

A6

Blackwell Dale
B6049

FB
1

START

2

Miller's Dale

4

Monsal Trail

N

Dismantled
Railway

B6049

Tideswell Dale

Ravenstor

High Dale

3

FB

Litton
Mill

Miller's Dale

Cressbrook

Cressbrook Dale

WALK 13

Water-cum-Jolly
Dale

0   ½   1

km (approx)

followed by a notice 'No through way ahead' as the line approaches the mouth of a tunnel.

3. Turn left here, as indicated, to descend the side of the embankment on a generally good path, fairly steeply through woodland. Go down a few steps and cross bridges over waterways at the former Litton Mill.

To view the considerable complex of the old site of Litton Mill, a diversion to the right, going a little further along the Monsal Trail, is necessary.

Otherwise, turn left to commence the return along the little riverside road, passing terraces of former mill workers' cottages. Pass the great rock face of Ravenstor, overhanging at the top and gouged out at the base.

4. Reach the Anglers Rest Inn. There is now a choice:

Either – walk to the road junction, bear left and continue for quarter of a mile along the main road, under the viaducts, to the junction with the Wormhill road. Turn right to rise steeply up to the turning into the car park.

Or – avoid the road walking by turning left along a signposted footpath immediately after passing the Anglers Rest. Cross two little bridges, then the main river on a longer bridge. At a 'Monsal Trail and Priestcliffe' signpost bear left to climb quite steeply up a reasonable path to join the Trail at point 2. Turn right to retrace the outward route to the former station and car park.

14. Ashford in the Water and Bakewell

Distance: 8.5km (5¼ miles)

Total ascent: 72m (236ft)

Start/car parking: Pay and display car park or roadside spaces at the former Bakewell railway station, grid reference 222690. From Bakewell town centre, cross the bridge over the River Wye and immediately fork right to drive uphill, direct to the station. Bakewell is well-provided with bus services, including the 171/181 to and from Chesterfield and Sheffield respectively.

Refreshments: Inns at Ashford. Café at the Country Bookstore, Hassop. Wide choice in Bakewell.

Map: 'White Peak' as for walk 5

About the Walk

The outward route follows yet another section of the trackbed of the former Midland Railway line – the Monsal Trail. The return has a mixture of paths and lanes, with almost half a mile by the side of A6020 to Ashford, followed by a path beside the River Wye. The final section into Bakewell is along the side of the A6. Entirely easy walking with only modest ascent, principally along the road when returning to the parking place.

Holme Bridge, Bakewell

Background

An entirely pleasant large village, Ashford in the Water is perhaps best known for the ancient Sheepwash Bridge which crosses the River Wye at the western end. Apart from the tower, most of the church was heavily restored in the 19th century. There are inns, an excellent café (the Cottage Tea Room) and a village store.

Bakewell is briefly described in walk 15.

The Walk

Pass to the left of the former station building.

1. Turn left to follow the trackbed of the former railway line, rising very gently. Pass the end of a terrace of four houses and under a stone bridge, then an open area with seat and picnic table. In little more than a mile, a gate on the right gives direct access to the Country Book Store, a large bookshop with café.

2. Continue along the trackbed, under a bridge, soon with more open views to the right – the part-wooded high ground is Longstone Edge. After public bridleways cross the Trail, go over a bridge.

3. 30m before the Trail goes over another road bridge, fork right, down a little path giving access to the road. Turn sharp left along the road, signposted 'Ashford, Baslow'. Join a more important road in 20m, passing under the old railway bridge. At the next junction, in 50m, go right, towards Ashford. Cross over and take the lane opposite, 'private road' with a 'public footpath' sign. Continue along the lane, steadily uphill initially. Over the top, pass Churchdale Lodge (farm/horse riding establishment) before reaching Churchdale Hall. Bear left to follow the signpost, to a gate/stile in 20m.

4. As the roadway bears to the left, go over a stile on the right, with 'public footpath' signpost. Stay fairly close to the right-hand boundary of the field, with the Hall to the right, reaching a waymarked stile over a stone wall. The path descends across a meadow to a stile over a fence, then more steeply to another stile over a fence in 50m. Go through woodland to a gate, cross a stream on a bridge and rise to a stile giving access to the A6020.

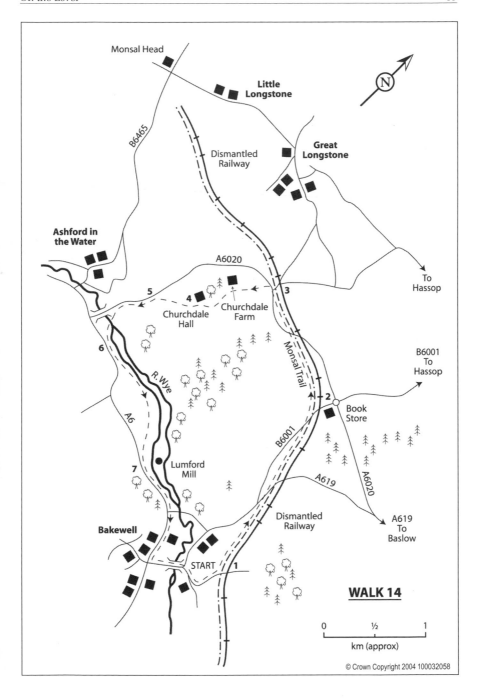

Monsal Head

Little Longstone

N

B6465

Dismantled Railway

Great Longstone

Ashford in the Water

A6020

To Hassop

5

4

3

Churchdale Hall

Churchdale Farm

6

R. Wye

Monsal Trail

B6001 To Hassop

A6

2

Book Store

B6001

7

Lumford Mill

A619

A6020

A619 To Baslow

Bakewell

Dismantled Railway

START

1

WALK 14

0   ½   1

km (approx)

© Crown Copyright 2004 100032058

5. Turn left to walk along the roadside footpath to Ashford.

In the village, the shop, inns and Sheepwash Bridge are all to the right.

The route to return to Bakewell goes to the left, along a surfaced lane, before the A6020 crosses the River Wye to join the A6. Pass a former mill site on the right, cross the river and join the A6.

6. Turn left. In 50m turn left again through a gate with a 'public footpath' sign. Follow the worn path over the grass, close to the river. There are occasional waymarks on posts as the path rises gently, soon with weirs in view. Go through two gates, then over a stile. After another stile the path goes between the gardens of houses. Cross a residential road to continue between more house gardens, then over a stile before bearing right to join the A6.

7. Turn left to walk by the roadside into Bakewell, about half a mile. To the left are the sites of historic mills.

A diversion of 40m is needed to visit Holme Bridge (packhorse) and the adjacent former sheepwash.

At the town centre roundabout, by the Rutland Arms, bear left past the public gardens. The road soon divides; either left or right leads to the main bridge. After the bridge, fork right to walk up the hill back to the former station and the car park.

15. Bakewell

Distance: 4.25km (2¾ miles)

Total ascent: 43m (141ft)

Start/car parking: Extensive pay and display car parks, both long and short stay, to the south-east of Bakewell Bridge, typical grid reference 221686. Bus services as for walk 14.

Refreshments: Wide choice in Bakewell.

Map: 'White Peak' as for walk 5.

About the Walk

An undemanding little circuit using grass paths along the bottom of the valley of the River Wye, with a return along the southern end of the Monsal Trail, along the trackbed of the former Midland railway line. There are no difficulties whatsoever. Good views over Bakewell and the valley from the railway embankment. One very short ascent up the side of the embankment.

Background

Bakewell has long been an important market town (charter 1330) and is now the largest settlement within the Peak District National Park. Market day each Monday attracts visi-

The Monsal Trail, near Bakewell

tors from far and wide, although redevelopment a few years ago of the former sprawling haphazard site has resulted in the loss of some of the original atmosphere. The early 18th-century market hall has been converted into a National Park and Tourist Information Centre.

Early aspirations to compete as a spa town with Buxton and Matlock never materialised.

Most important historically is the parish church, still displaying many Norman features and a rich variety of monuments including an 8th-century Saxon cross and a large collection of ancient tombstones and coffins.

Several wells are 'dressed' each year in accordance with the ancient pagan Peak District tradition, giving thanks for the vital, life-sustaining, water. Well dressing has subsequently been adapted as a Christian ceremony, first recorded at Tissington in 1758.

Well provided with shops, inns, cafés and other modern facilities, the compact and lively town centre also has many fine buildings, including an old house converted into a local museum.

Today, Bakewell's widespread fame rests on more slender foundations – the Bakewell 'tart' – made throughout the land both commercially and by home baking. Local people will quickly point out that the 'tart' is not the genuine article. Happily, local bakers do still make and sell the real thing – Bakewell 'pudding' – a clearly superior confection.

The Walk

Adjacent to the car park is a large building with an odd-shaped roof. From the car park walk towards this building. Cross a little bridge.

1. Turn right, along a surfaced footpath leading to the entrance to Bakewell show ground, with a cattle grid and a little gate. Follow the road through the extensive show ground. As the road bends to the right, go straight ahead to a waymark on a gatepost and a stile in 40m. Continue along a path by the left edge of a meadow, with a fence on the left. Go through/over another gate/stile in 100m. Carry on as before; the path is a little vague. Pass a 'public footpath' signpost and angle across a meadow to the right-hand of two openings in the hedge ahead, with gate and waymark on post. Cross a bridge over a ditch and turn right (waymark on post) to head for a waymarked gate with a four-way signpost beyond.

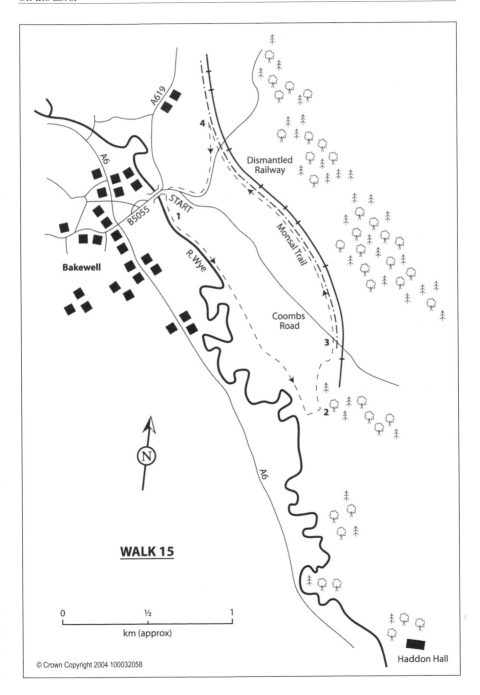

Bakewell

Dismantled
Railway

Monsal Trail

Coombs
Road

R. Wye

START

A619

A6

B5055

N

WALK 15

0   ½   1

km (approx)

© Crown Copyright 2004 100032058

A6

Haddon Hall

2. Go through and turn left for 'public bridleway, Coombs Road', rising gently along the left edge of a rough pasture. Go through the signposted gate at the top and turn left along a lane, now with good views over the valley of the River Wye. Join a surfaced lane (Coombs Road), with a former railway viaduct to the right. Turn left for 20m then turn right up a steep path with some steps to reach the trackbed of the former railway line, at the southern extremity of the Monsal Trail.

3. Turn left; there are helpful information boards. The track rises gently, first on embankment, then in cutting. Go under a skewed stone bridge, then another stone bridge before reaching the former Bakewell station, again with an interesting information board.

4. Turn left at the far end of the building, cross the old station yard, pass the former weighbridge building opposite, bearing left then right to walk downhill towards the town centre. At the bottom turn left into Coombs Road, then right to return to the car park.

16. Longnor

Distance: 6km (3¼ miles)

Total ascent: 149m (489ft) Using the road out of Longnor as an alternative start as far as point 3 reduces this to 116m (381ft).

Start/car parking: Parking area in the centre of Longnor, grid reference 089650. Bus services to Longnor include the 458 from Leek and Hanley, operated by Aimee's Travel.

Refreshments: Four inns and two tea shops in Longnor (also a fish and chip shop!).

Map: 'White Peak' as for walk 5.

About the Walk

This is a walk set largely in the valley of the upper part of the River Dove. As Longnor is situated on a ridge of high ground, inevitably there is a down and then up configuration. The ascent on the return is quite steep, fortunately for a comparatively short distance. Lanes and good paths comprise the majority of the route, with a short distance by the side of the B5063 road (increased to rather more than a mile if the alternative route is used). There are fine views of some of the most shapely limestone hills.

Background

Sometimes described as a miniature town, Longnor does have four inns and a few shops in its tight-knit central area at the meeting place of the 18th-century turnpike roads which cross the extensive surrounding moorland. The ridge on which the village stands separates the upper valleys of the Dove and Manifold rivers.

The upper part of the valley of the River Dove comprises agreeable farmland, entirely different from the spectacular scenery of the celebrated Dovedale a few miles downstream. The adjacent Chrome Hill and Parkhouse Hill are, however, most impressive sharp peaks. Between these two hills is Dowel Dale; a diversion of half a mile (uphill!) from the route of this walk, along a minor road, leads to a cave used by stone age hunter/gatherers. Ten skeletons were unearthed during excavations.

The Walk

From the central parking area walk to the Horseshoe Inn. Turn right towards Buxton at the road junction, now with the inn on the left.

1. In less than 100m, turn right into Church Street, then turn left at once to rise up a surfaced lane with a cul-de-sac sign. In 100m go right, up the banking, on a just-visible path, to a stile on the left, with a waymark on a post. Cross the gardens of a pair of semi-detached bungalows, then go over a stile, to continue along the right edge of a field, with a wall on the right. Go over a waymarked stile.

   The valley of the River Dove is now in view, with Chrome Hill, Parkhouse Hill, Hitter Hill and Wheeldon Hill beyond.

The unmistakeable reef edges of Parkhouse and Chrome Hill

   Descend the scarp through light woodland, passing a waymark on a post, to reach a signpost and a squeezer stile/gate. Join a farm access track, continuing to the entrance to a pair of houses in 150m.

2. Turn right here, along a broad, rough, track, soon joining a surfaced roadway close to Yewtree Grange Farm. Turn left,

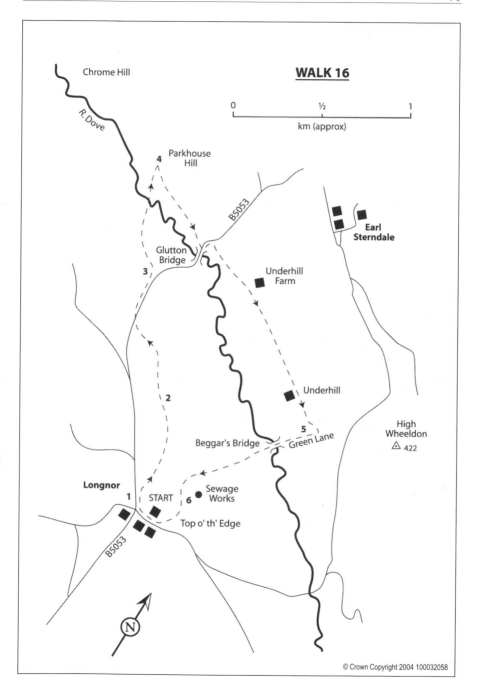

Chrome Hill

R. Dove

WALK 16

0   ½   1
km (approx)

Parkhouse
Hill
4

B5053

Earl
Sterndale

Glutton
Bridge
3

Underhill
Farm

2

Underhill

5

High
Wheeldon
△ 422

Beggar's Bridge   Green Lane

Longnor
1   START   6   Sewage
Works
Top o' th' Edge

B5053

N

© Crown Copyright 2004 100032058

uphill, to join the public road. Turn right, to walk downhill by the roadside for about 300m, passing 'High Acres'. *(The alternative route to point 3, reducing the ascent, is to walk by the roadside along the B5063 from the crossroads in Longnor.)*

3. Turn left at a gate/stile with 'footpath' sign, along a lane, rising a little. Pass a house then, in 150m, as the lane turns into the grounds of another house, go straight ahead through a gate. Go through a squeezer stile in 60m to follow a path descending across rough pasture to a footbridge over the infant River Dove. Continue the same line across further rough pasture, to a little gate giving access to a surfaced lane below Parkhouse Hill. Dowel Dale is ahead.

4. Turn right to walk along the lane to a junction with B5063. Turn left to Glutton Bridge, then turn right in 60m along a surfaced lane 'unsuitable for motors', a fine walking route low across the valley side. Underhill Farm (one of three of the same name in this part of the valley!) is to the left. Go straight ahead through a gate. After another gate, pass a house, then go through another gate. Carry on, the lane now losing its tarmac surface. After yet another gate in 100m, approach (another) Underhill Farm. There are more gates and a waymark, showing the route through the farmyard. Continue along the farm access drive.

5. As the roadway bends sharply to the left, turn right, to a signposted ('Longnor') gate/stile and a green lane leading to Beggar's Bridge, over the River Dove. Continue the same line, quite steeply up a sloping meadow; the gradient soon eases. Head for a solitary farm building. Pass to the right of the building. Turn left at a 'public bridleway' sign to join a sewage works access drive, angling up the steep scarp. Go through/over a gate/stile before reaching the top, close to houses – 'Top o' th' Edge' – the fringe of Longnor.

6. Turn left at the surfaced road, to a junction in 100m. Carry on along a walled lane, passing a residential development, descending towards the village centre. Go right at the next junction, then left in 15m to join the main street. Turn right to pass the Cheshire Cheese Inn and return to the parking area.

17. Monyash and Lathkill Dale

Distance: 6.5km (4 miles)

Total ascent: 120m (394ft)

Start/car parking: Small car park in Monyash, in Chapel Street, almost opposite the Methodist chapel, grid reference 150667.

Refreshments: Inn and café in Monyash.

Map: 'White Peak' as for walk 5.

About the Walk

A classic Peak District walk, crossing an upland agricultural area before descending into Cales Dale, then returning along the bottom of the upper part of the celebrated Lathkill Dale. The great majority of the ascent occurs in the steady upward plod from the footbridge in Lathkill Dale, all at a reasonable gradient. There are very short sections with rock underfoot but otherwise the route comprises a fine mixture of lanes and paths, with roadside walking confined to about half a mile on the return to Monyash.

Background

Monyash is a typical Peak District village, with all the essentials – church, inn, café and store – set attractively around a little green, with the shaft of an old cross. Originally of about 1200, the church has been much restored over the ensuing centuries, although some of the tower is still 13th century.

Lathkill Dale is justifiably regarded as one of the finest in the National Park, with abundant rock scenery and with some areas protected by English Nature.

The Walk

Start from the car park in Monyash and walk back to the village centre, by the café and the inn (both very welcoming to walkers).

1. Go straight across the main road, to follow Raikes Road for about a quarter of a mile. As the road bends to the right, uphill, go straight ahead, along a broad track. Take the left fork in 50m ('public footpath' signpost), an unsurfaced track rising gently

between limestone walls. Go through/over a gate/stile and continue, with a wall on the right, as far as a National Trust 'Fern Dale' sign.

2. Turn right here to a stile over the wall ('public footpath' sign), cross a little field to another signposted stile and carry on across the bottom of tiny Fern Dale. Go through a squeezer stile to a 'public footpath, Youlgreave' sign. Carry on, uphill, with a wall on the left, to a gate/stile at the top. Continue to a signposted and waymarked stile on the left. Keep the same line, now with the wall on the right, downhill, to a farm gate on the right. Go through and follow the farm access lane to the large and historic farmstead of One Ash Grange.

3. Among the farm buildings look carefully for the 'public footpath' sign on a wall and turn left before a terrace of cottages, passing behind the cottages to reach a fork. Go right here (waymark on post) to a mini squeezer stile and a few steep steps down. Follow the obvious path along the bottom edge of a field, descending into Cales Dale. Go through a gate with an English Nature notice, entering light woodland. There is a short steep, rocky section of path and a tunnel to the right. At a signposted junction go straight on, following the narrow but adequate path along the bottom of the dale, with cliffs on the far side of Lathkill Dale in view ahead.

4. Reach the junction of the dales at a stile, footbridge and dry river bed. There is an information board. Cross the bridge and turn left to follow the path up the bottom of Lathkill Dale, rising steadily for a little more than two miles in total. The path is always easy to follow. At a junction of dales bear left, the rock scenery now becoming more spectacular. Pass an English Nature information board explaining the rare flowers (Jacob's Ladder) in adjacent land before rising to a squeezer stile through a wall and entering light woodland. The path now winds among rocks, with a great deal of spoil as evidence of former mining and quarrying in this area. Leave the dale through a kissing gate, rising over grass to a gate/stile in 70 yards. Continue to another kissing gate, then along a well-used track over grass to a kissing gate and the public road, by a 'Lathkill Dale' information board.

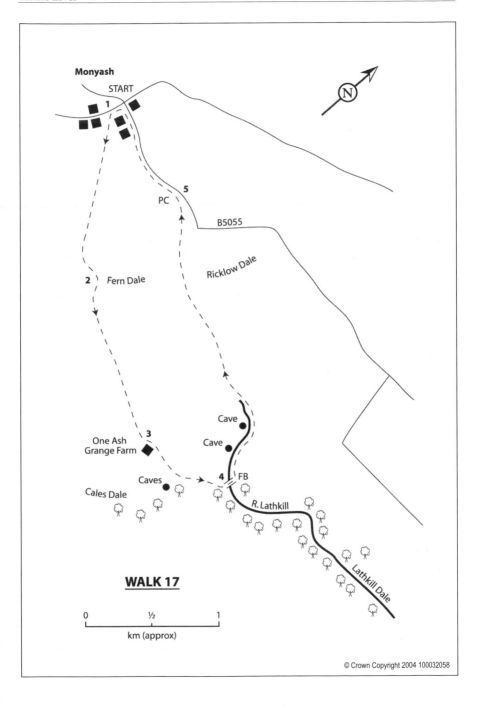

Monyash

START

1

2 ⟩ Fern Dale

5

PC

B5055

Ricklow Dale

Cave

3
One Ash
Grange Farm

Cave

Caves

4 ⟍ FB

Cales Dale

R. Lathkill

Lathkill Dale

N

WALK 17

0   ½   1

km (approx)

5. Turn left to walk uphill by the roadside, passing a camping site, then attractive cottages, the village store, St Leonard's church on the left, sympathetic modern housing, the inn and the café, before turning right at Chapel Street to return to the car park.

The Bull's Head, Monyash with café beyond

18. Middleton by Youlgreave and Alport

Distance: 3.5km (2¼ miles)

Total ascent: Negligible.

Start/car parking: Roadside spaces on the edges of the large open area in Middleton village, grid reference 196632. There are public conveniences adjacent and this area is also the terminus of the bus service. After this linear walk, use the Hulleys 171/181 bus service, basically 2 hourly, (1 hourly at weekends), to return. An alternative is to park at Alport (lay-bys on both sides of the road), catch the bus to Middleton, and walk back.

Refreshments: Meadow Cottage tea shop, Youlgreave.

Map: 'White Peak' as for walk 5.

About the Walk

A gentle walk along Bradford Dale, with virtually no ascent, all on excellent tracks.

Background

The charming hamlet of Alport is at the junction of Lathkill and Bradford Dales, with the site of a former mill, bridges and old cottages clustered by the water.

Middleton by Youlgreave is a quiet agricultural backwater, with attractive cottages spread around the large central open area.

Youlgreave, close to the line of this walk, is a large, linear, village with a church, inns and other facilities. There are houses of the early 17th century and the church has some surviving Norman work and a 15th-century tower. The east window has glass by the pre-Raphaelites, Burne-Jones and William Morris. The font is 12th century. A short distance along the main street from the church is the conduit head of 1829, a 1500-gallon water tank supplied from a spring at Morstone, for many years the village water supply. The adjacent striking former Co-operative store building is now a youth hostel.

Alport

The Walk

Leave the central area of Middleton along a surfaced road opposite the children's play area and descend gently to start the walk.

1. The road loses its surface; bear left, still downhill, at a 'public footpath' sign. There are soon rock faces on either side, forming a mini dale. At the bottom of the slope the track bears to the left, along the bottom of Bradford Dale, here well-wooded. The stream usually has very little water in this section. Reach a bridge, with a junction of footpaths, a signpost and a waymark. Go straight on; the River Bradford now has much more water. Go through a gate; there is an interesting construction of a wall over the river, which has a long series of dams and ponds.

2. Go through a gate, cross the river on a clapper bridge, turn right immediately through a gate/squeezer stile with 'Limestone Way' signpost, and continue, with the river now on the right.

    Meadow Cottage tea shop is visible, just a few metres up the lane.

    Go through a waymarked gate to reach a public road, on the fringe of Youlgreave. Go straight ahead, across the front of a terrace of four cottages.

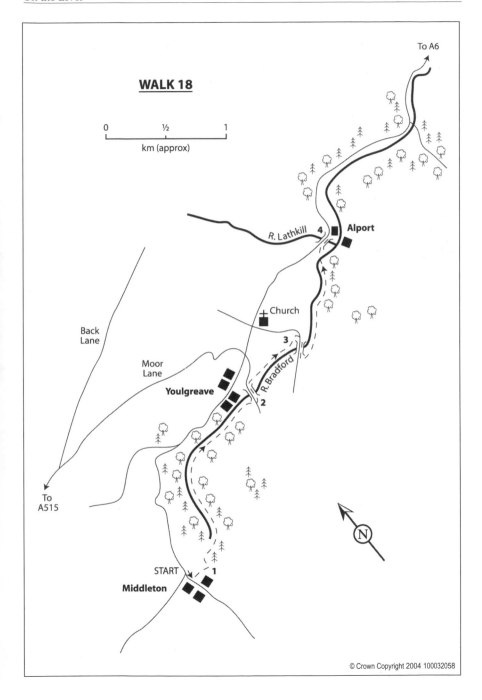

WALK 18

0   ½   1
km (approx)

To A6

R. Lathkill   4   ■ **Alport**
■

+ Church
■

Back
Lane

Moor
Lane   3

■
Youlgreave   ■
■   2   R. Bradford

To
A515

N

START   1
Middleton   ■
■

© Crown Copyright 2004 100032058

3. Do not cross the river; go straight ahead through a waymarked gate ('Haddon Estate Private Road') along an unsurfaced roadway. Cross the river, soon passing a lovely old (packhorse?) bridge on the left. Do not cross the bridge. Continue along the roadway until, as it bears to the right, uphill, go through a gate/stile on the left to stay close to the river, with two more gates before the public road is reached at Alport.

4. For the return bus, turn right, by the roadside, for less than 100m. Do not cross the road. The bus for Middleton stops opposite the official bus stop on the far side of the road (wave to the driver). *If the vehicle has been parked at Alport, the roadside areas are a few metres to the left from point 4.*

19. Stanton Moor

Distance: 4km (2½ miles)

Total ascent: 50m (164ft)

Start/car parking: Informal lay-by, half a mile north of Birchover village, by the side of the road to Stanton in Peak, grid reference 242628.

Refreshments: None en route. Inns at Stanton and Birchover.

Map: 'White Peak' as for walk 5.

About the Walk

A fine straightforward ramble around Stanton Moor, with only a small amount of ascent, none steep or prolonged. The footpaths are excellent.

Background

Stanton Moor is a relatively small area of gritstone isolated within the generally limestone countryside of the 'White Peak'. Silver birch, rhododendron and heather are all indicators of the underlying geology. Stanton Moor Edge, overlooking the broad valley of the River Derwent, is a typically steep gritstone scarp, with tors and other rock features, much of it covered by woodland. The area of land including the Edge is in the ownership of the National Trust.

The Reform Tower, Stanton Moor

Many burial mounds, standing stones and the Nine Ladies stone circle provide evidence of extensive occupation of the Moor during the early Bronze Age. In more recent times, extensive quarrying has left its mark, particularly along the western fringe; fortunately, nature is fast reclaiming these devastated areas.

Above Stanton Moor Edge is a stone tower, erected by Early Grey in 1832 to commemorate the passage of his great Parliamentary Reform Bill. The route along the top of the Edge has fine view over a wide swathe of the valley of the River Derwent.

Stanton and Birchover are modestly attractive hillside villages, each with good cottages and an inn.

The Walk

Leave the road along a broad track, passing a large horizontal stone and rising to a stile in less than 50m. Continue, reaching the massive Cork Stone in a short distance.

1. Turn left by the stone, then fork left in 50m to follow a clear path across heather moorland. Pass through light woodland (silver birch), with extensive old quarry workings on the left. At various forks stay with the main track, never far from a fence on the left. At a cross-path by the corner of a fence, go straight ahead with the fence now very close on the left. At a farm-type gate, turn right, along a broad track, descending gently.

2. Join the main track across the moor, turning right. The Nine Ladies stone circle is on the right in about 200m, with the King's Stone not far away. Opposite the stone circle turn left along a minor path heading directly towards the Reform Tower. Keep left at a fork in 150m to reach the tower, over a stile.

3. Turn right, by the side of the tower, to follow a little path, descending through bracken. Another path joins from the left in a few metres. The track soon levels and wends its way delightfully along the top of Stanton Moor Edge, perched high above the River Derwent, with extensive views over the valley.

There are several short diversions to tors and viewpoints.

4. Opposite a great boulder, with a National Trust 'Stanton Moor Edge' sign, turn right to leave the path over a stile. Take a left fork

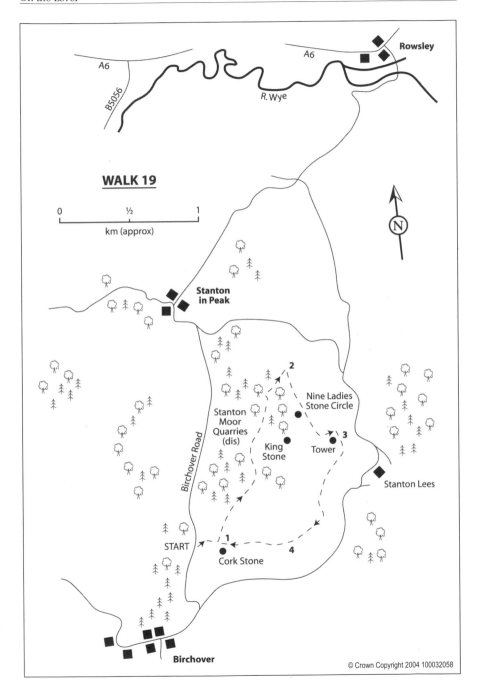

WALK 19

0   ½   1

km (approx)

N

A6

B5056

R. Wye

Rowsley

Stanton
in Peak

Birchover Road

Stanton
Moor
Quarries
(dis)

2

Nine Ladies
Stone Circle

King
Stone

3

Tower

Stanton Lees

START

1

Cork Stone

4

Birchover

© Crown Copyright 2004 100032058

at once, soon reaching the main path across the moor. Go straight across to a very minor path, rising steadily at a reasonable gradient. Join a more major track, bearing left to reach the Cork Stone. Rejoin the outward route to return to the parking area.

20. Hartington

Distance: 9.5km (6 miles)

Total ascent: 112m (368ft)

Start/car parking: Pay and display car park close to the village centre, grid reference 128604, or roadside parking spaces. Bus services include the 171/181 to and from Chesterfield and Sheffield and the 458 to and from Leek and Hanley.

Refreshments: Two inns and three tea shops in Hartington.

Map: 'White Peak' as for walk 5.

About the Walk

One of the longer walks in the book, this delightful circuit includes Biggin Dale, Wolfscote Dale and Beresford Dale. There is a fair amount of ascent, mostly towards the end, rising from Beresford Dale back to Hartington, at a generally easy gradient. Lanes and footpaths provide first class walking surfaces. There is, however, some stony ground underfoot in Biggin Dale

Background

The spacious village of Hartington has a duck pond, shops, inns and tea shops. Of particular interest is a small shop with a big reputation selling locally made 'blue' cheese. The church is mainly of the 14th century, with older fragments. Hartington Hall, a fine gabled building was built in the 16th century and restored in the 19th. It has been used for many years as a youth hostel.

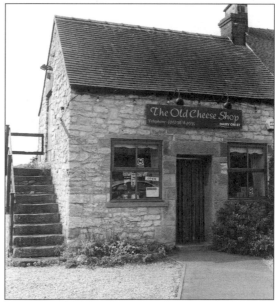

The famous cheese shop at Hartington

Although close together, the three dales have quite different characters. Beresford Dale and Wolfscote Dale are contiguous sections of the valley of the River Dove, the former heavily wooded, with exposed limestone cliffs and the latter more open, with great swathes of scree on the valley sides. Biggin Dale is a 'dry' dale, otherwise more akin to Wolfscote Dale in character.

Close to the exit from Beresford Dale, on the left almost concealed by trees, is Charles Cotton's fishing lodge, a small building erected in 1674 as a base for his local fishing excursions with his great friend Izaak Walton (famous for his book, 'The Compleat Angler'). Cotton owned the nearby Beresford Hall and was noted for his ability to avoid creditors. In the grounds is a cave in which he is reputed to have hidden from time to time.

The Walk

From the middle of Hartington, by the bus shelter, walk along the road towards Newhaven, B5054, passing a general store and reaching a junction in 100m.

1. Turn right at the junction, signposted 'Youth Hostel' for a steep ascent on a minor road. Pass the Old Chapel and turn right in 30m for 'Wolfscote Grange Farm', still rising. The gradient soon eases, followed by level walking along a lane across typical upland 'white peak' agricultural countryside. Pass farm buildings.

    The hills to the right include Narrowdale and Ecton. At the next junction, a little lane to the right signposted 'Beresford and Wolfscote Dale' provides a short walk option. Keep straight ahead for the full walk.

2. At a junction the surfaced road bends sharply to the right. Go straight on, signposted 'Biggin Dale' along an unsurfaced lane between stone walls, soon reaching a large isolated farm building. Go through over a gate/stile. After more gate/stiles, the track descends towards Biggin Dale, gently at first but with a short steep section over grass at the end, passing a ruined building to reach the dale bottom. There is a 'public bridleway to Biggin Dale' signpost.

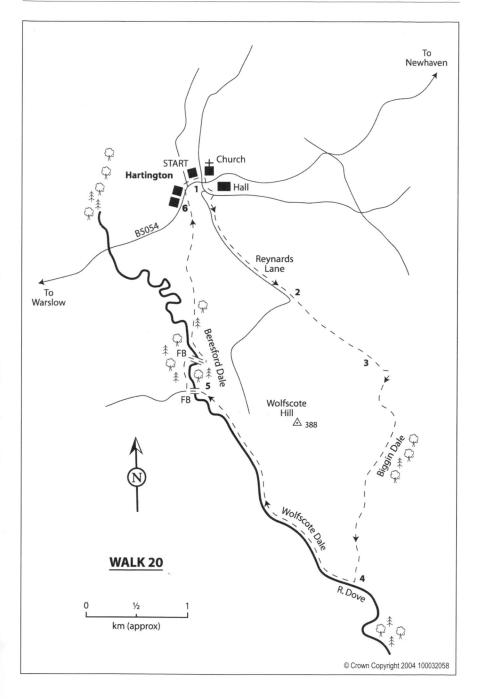

To Newhaven

START

Hartington

Church

Hall

6

B5054

To Warslow

Reynards Lane

2

3

Beresford Dale

FB

5

FB

Wolfscote Hill
△ 388

Biggin Dale

N

Wolfscote Dale

WALK 20

0   ½   1
km (approx)

4

R. Dove

© Crown Copyright 2004 100032058

3. Turn right over the short-cropped grass. Bear left at a wood to rise to a gate, with a dewpond on the right. At a 'public bridleway to Biggin Dale' signpost in 20m, turn right to continue, with a stone wall on the right.

A National Nature Reserve board gives information on local flora and fauna, particularly noting the gorse, which is generally rare in the limestone dales.

Go through a gate with National Trust sign. The path is now stony with some (ash) woodland. Go through another gate, into more woodland, soon with the impressive Peaseland Rocks in Wolfscote Dale in view ahead.

4. Join a made-up path in Wolfscote Dale. Turn right to walk beside the River Dove, rising gently along the bottom of the dale. There are many weirs, with fine rock scenery, including Drabber Tor on the left, and riverside trees. Go through a gate/squeezer stile by a National Trust 'Wolfscote Dale' sign. Go through another gate/squeezer stile. There is a bridge on the left and a lane to the right. Do not cross the bridge. Continue to a stile in 40m and cross a meadow on a well-worn track.

5. Go through a squeezer stile, cross a footbridge or stepping stones across the river.

To the left is a surfaced lane and the entrance to Beresford House.

Turn right to continue along heavily wooded Beresford Dale, now with the river on the right. Pike Pool, with its rock pinnacle, is a few metres before another footbridge. Cross, soon rising through light woodland to leave the dale at a stile. Follow the path across a meadow, rising across the shoulder of shapely Penn's Low.

At the high point, look back to see Charles Cotton's fishing house among the trees.

Go through a gateway ('public footpath' sign) then rise again steadily across fields, through a signposted gap in a wall. There are waymarks on posts before a gate and stile are reached. Cross a tiny lane to a waymarked gate and stile and a made-up path to a gate by the side of the public conveniences.

One of the old footpath society signs is in front of the conveniences.

6. Turn right at the public road to return to the village centre (or cross the road to the car park).

21. Rudyard Lake

Distance: 7.25km (4½ miles)

Total ascent: 61m (200ft)

Start/car parking: Informal parking area at the north end of the lake, grid reference 939611. Turn west off A523 Macclesfield to Leek road at a minor road leading to Rycroft Gate. In less than 200m, immediately after crossing the former railway bridge, turn left along an unsurfaced roadway. The parking area is almost half a mile along this roadway, at a junction. The tourist information centre in Leek has details of the bus services in this area.

Refreshments: Café at south end of lake.

Map: 'White Peak' as for walk 5.

About the Walk

A circuit of the attractive Rudyard Lake, with comparatively little ascent, all at very easy gradients. Much of the outward route is along good tracks and roadways included in the designated Staffordshire Way and Staffordshire Moorland Walks, with the return along the trackbed of the former Macclesfield to Leek railway line.

Background

Although strictly a reservoir, Rudyard Lake is a very attractive expanse of water, with fishing, boat hire and other water-based leisure activities, encouraged. At the south end is a modest visitor complex, with café.

Based on the old station site to the south of the lake, The Rudyard Lake Steam Railway, an 11"-gauge miniature railway, operates services along almost two miles of the trackbed of the former railway. Timetables are displayed.

The Walk

From the parking area turn right (signpost and 'Staffordshire Way' mark). Go along the unsurfaced roadway, passing another signpost/waymark in 100m. Cross a stone bridge over a stream in a further few metres and continue along a private road, now tarmac

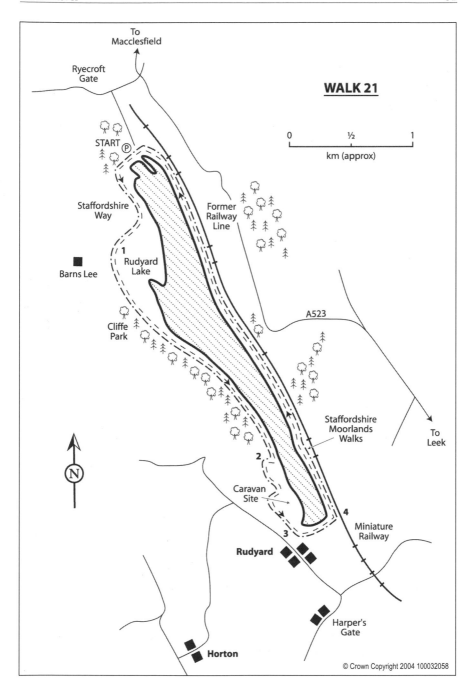

To
Macclesfield

Ryecroft
Gate

WALK 21

0   ½   1
km (approx)

START (P)

Staffordshire
Way

Former
Railway
Line

1
Rudyard
Lake

Barns Lee

Cliffe
Park

A523

Staffordshire
Moorlands
Walks

To
Leek

2

Caravan
Site

4

Miniature
Railway

3

Rudyard

Harper's
Gate

Horton

N

© Crown Copyright 2004 100032058

surfaced, signposted to Barns Lee Farm and Cliffe Park Hall. After a waymarked gate/stile, the road bends to the right, away from the lakeshore, rising gently across farmland.

1. Just before reaching a belt of trees, fork left to leave the road; there are hard wheel tracks. Pass a waymark on a post in 50m and enter woodland, still rising gently. Reach the battlemented Cliffe Park Hall, formerly a youth hostel. Go through a gate and over a cattle grid to pass in front of the Hall. Exit by a waymarked gate (concessionary footpath) at the far end and continue along a broad track, gently downhill. Go through or over a waymarked gate and stile, again in woodland. Pass a boating club with modern building on the left and a solid stone former lodge on the right. The roadway becomes tarmac surfaced.

2. Less than 50m after a right-hand bend, look for a path on the left, quite narrow but very clear, with signpost and 'Staffordshire Way' mark. Follow the path to a signposted junction with another path. Turn left. Join a surfaced access roadway. Turn right, uphill. Pass a three-way signpost then, after less than 100m on the concrete roadway, fork left along a waymarked narrow path. Go left at a junction in 50m or so, passing above a

By the shore of Rudyard Lake

caravan site. At a junction of unsurfaced roadways go straight ahead, passing the backs of terraces of houses to reach the end of a surfaced road. The Crescent is to the left.

3. Walk along the road, with houses on the right, for 100m. Turn left along a signposted footpath, just before a major car park. Go through a little gate to descend to the visitor area on the lake shore; facilities include a café and public conveniences. Continue across the top of the dam.

4. Join the trackbed of the former railway line. Turn left to carry on along this wide easy track, with miniature railway, passing Lakeside Station, Hunt House Wood Station (terminus) and then through a vehicular gate. Pass a boating club premises with pedestrian overbridge. Go under a stone bridge before returning to the parking area.

22. Tittesworth

Distance: 4km (2½ miles)

Total ascent: 35m (115ft)

Start/car parking: Extensive pay and display car parking areas at Tittesworth Visitor Centre, grid reference 994604. On Sundays and Bank Holidays there is a park and ride bus service to and from the nearby Staffordshire Roaches.

Refreshments: Café at Visitor Centre. Lazy Trout Inn at Merebrook.

Map: 'White Peak' as for walk 5.

About the Walk

A gentle rural ramble using part of the designated Staffordshire Moorland Walks and a minor road to form a circuit based on the substantial modern complex of the Tittesworth Visitor Centre (Severn Trent Water Authority). Not all sections of footpath are distinct on the ground and there are numerous stiles and gates, generally well-waymarked.

Background

The Visitor Centre includes an information display, shop, café and toilets. Outside, children's play area, barbeque, bird watching information and a nature trail are all provided.

Merebrook is a quietly attractive village with parish church and the Lazy Trout Inn.

The excellent Visitor Centre

The Walk

Go back along the visitor centre access drive to the public road.

1. Turn right to walk by the roadside for one third of a mile.

    There are good views of the long ridge of the Roaches and the adjacent Hen Cloud.

    As the road bends strongly to the right, go over a waymarked stile on the left. Follow a path across a meadow to a waymarked gate. Cross a bridge over a ditch and continue to another waymarked bridge and gate in 40m. Cross a meadow to a waymarked gate with an unusual orange disc on a pole. Carry on along a better path to a disc and a waymark on a post. Turn right to walk up the left edge of a field, towards Benthead. In 150m turn left, over a waymarked bridge with a gate at each end and follow a clear path to a plank bridge and a stile with waymark and disc. Descend gently across a rough meadow to a waymarked gate. Continue along the top edge of a very large pasture, with a fence on the right.

2. On reaching a stile on the right, turn left to head for an isolated farm building, descending gently. Go over a waymarked stile at the side of the building and carry on across the next pasture, still descending, to a waymarked stile, then a signpost. Turn right, to head for 'Frith Bottom'. Go over a stile beside a gate and continue, bearing a little to the right; there is no clear path here and the ground is cattle-churned. Pass a signpost, still heading for 'Frith Bottom'. Go over a stile with 'Moorland Walk' waymark. Walk along wooden decking, beside trees, with Frith Bottom (farm) to the right.

3. Go over a stile and join the farm access track. Turn left, cross a stream and rise gently to a gate/cattle grid. Turn left at once at a signpost, cross a little field to a gate, then a stile in less than 50m, passing a waymarked signpost, then along the right edge of a little field and through old stone gateposts; there is a waymark on a post. Go over a signposted/waymarked stile on the right and pass the end of a house to a waymark on a post. Bear right, across the front of the house 'Lower Lee' to a lane leading to the public road.

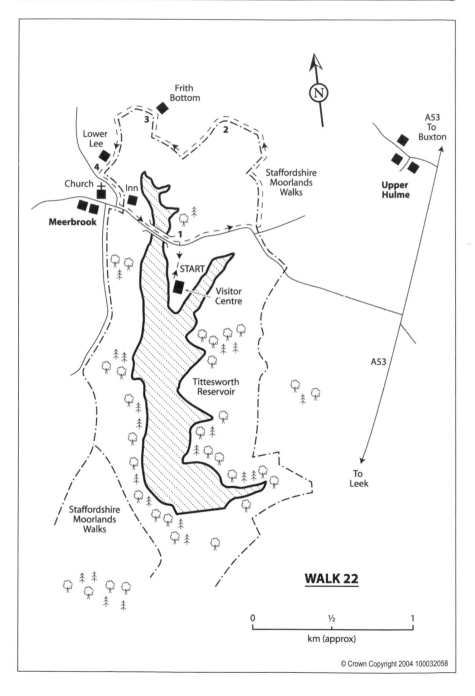

WALK 22

4. Turn left to walk to Merebrook, with the church to the right and the Lazy Trout Inn on the left. Turn left at the road junction, continuing past the Methodist chapel to cross the bridge over the reservoir before turning right to return to the visitor centre and car parks.

23. Alstonefield

Distance: 5km (3 miles)

Total ascent: 95m (312ft)

Start/car parking: Small car park by the public conveniences in Alstonefield, grid reference 131556.

Refreshments: Inns at Alstonefield and Wetton.

Map: 'White Peak' as for walk 5.

About the Walk

A straightforward rural ramble connecting two villages using a series of field paths, mostly good and not difficult to follow. There are many stiles, including some 'squeezers'. The route crosses a valley in each direction. The total ascent, therefore, occurs in two parts, that approaching Wetton being steeper than the return, although neither is difficult or prolonged.

Background

Alstonefield is a lovely village, with the trim green perfectly placed in front of the popular George Inn. An equally trim village, Wetton has Ye Olde Royal Oak as its focal point.

The countryside between the two villages is pleasantly rolling upland set between the two celebrated valleys – the Dove and the Manifold.

The Walk

Turn right from the car park to follow a narrow path for a few metres up to the road. Turn right, and then:

1. At a road junction in 100m turn right, cross the road and continue along a stone surfaced lane with a 'public footpath' signpost at the left side of the Memorial Hall. Pass a children's play area and along the edge of a football field, keeping close to the boundary fence/wall on the right. Go over a stile in the far corner. Cross the next field on an obvious path, slightly diagonal, downhill to a signposted squeezer stile to continue to a sign-

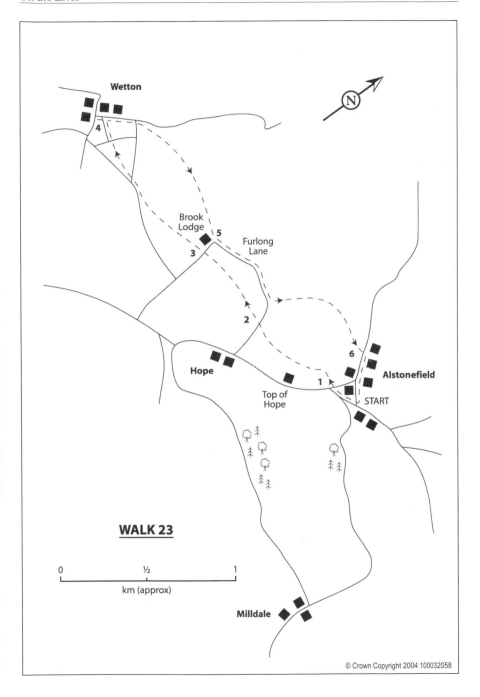

Wetton

Brook
Lodge

5

Furlong
Lane

4

3

2

Hope

Top of
Hope

1

6

Alstonefield

START

WALK 23

0   ½   1

km (approx)

Milldale

posted stile and a minor public road. The 'Top of Hope' hamlet is to the left.

2. Cross the road to a squeezer stile and carry on, aiming for the end of a stone wall, still descending gently. Go straight ahead at a signposted gate/stile/gate. Cross the valley bottom, go through an old squeezer stile, then a waymarked kissing gate and cross a paddock with a house to the right. Go through another waymarked gate/stile, cross a small field to a waymarked gate, with a cottage on the right, to rise across a small field to a squeezer stile.

3. Cross the little road again, go through a signposted squeezer stile and rise across a larger field.

    Narrowdale Hill is in view to the right.

    By the side of a cattle-drinking trough go over the end of a wall (a stile appears to have been obliterated). Go through a squeezer stile, then along the left edge of a meadow with a stone wall on the left before angling up to a squeezer stile giving access to a public road. Turn right, still rising gently. Ignore a road on the right in 100m. Go over a stile on the right in 50m after the junction to follow a little path, over a stile on the left in 100m then two more stiles to join a village road. Turn right to rise to Wetton village centre, with tiny triangular green, seats and Ye Olde Royal Oak.

4. Return along the same road but keep straight on at the road junction. At the next road junction, in about 250m look for a footpath sign and go through a little gate, opposite. Descend across a rough pasture; the path is not well-defined. Aim for the bottom right corner and a waymarked stile. Go through a waymarked gate in 70m then bear right across more rough pasture to a squeezer stile/gateway. Go over a stile to join a green lane between stone walls. Turn right to walk to the public road, Furlong Lane, by Brook Lodge.

5. Turn left to walk along the lane for a third of a mile. At a point where there are footpaths to right and left, turn left over a stile to follow a footpath gently rising, close to the wall on the left, soon with the northern fringe of Alstonefield in view ahead. Go over a

stile and continue with the wall now on the right. Go through a waymarked gate, bear right to a gate/stile, and follow a walled lane up to the public road.

6. Turn right to walk by the roadside back to Alstonefield.

Note the 'Green Well', a former village water supply, in a stone enclosure to the right.

At a junction, stay with the main road, slightly left, to the car park and public conveniences. For the inn and the village centre, continue past the car park for a short distance.

Alstonefield's former water supply

24. Manifold Valley

Distance: 6km (3¾ miles)

Total ascent: 15m (49ft)

Start/car parking: Parking area at Weag's Bridge, grid reference 100542. Accessed by a minor road from Grindon, signposted 'Manifold Valley' or from Wetton/Alstonefield.

Refreshments: Teas, ices and light refreshments at Wettonmill.

Map: 'White Peak' as for walk 5.

About the Walk

Entirely easy, straightforward walking, out and back along a former railway line. Minimal ascent and excellent underfoot.

Background

Second only to Dovedale as a popular and attractive Peak District valley, the Manifold has limestone crags, caves and other features in a well-wooded landscape. Of particular significance is Thor's Cave, a great gash in an impressively steep rock, which provided shelter for 'cavemen', hunter/gatherers of the Stone Age. Unfortunately, Victorian excavations were less than scientific and much of the historic material was not properly recorded. A smaller cave at Wettonmill was similarly used by hunter/gatherers. Thor's Cave can be reached by a short (but very steep) diversion from the route of this walk.

The Manifold is probably the best known case of the Peak District phenomenon of a disappearing river or stream. The riverbed becomes dry just below Wettonmill, with no noticeable reappearance until the grounds of Ilam Hall, several miles downstream.

The use of the trackbed of the former Leek and Manifold Valley Light Railway has long been a great facility for walkers and cyclists. Built in 1904 to the unusual gauge of 2' 6", this over optimistic line connected the North Staffordshire Railway at Waterhouses with the tiny village of Hulme End. The intermediate villages are situated high above the valley sides, well away from the line, and the valley itself has minimal population. Consequently, trade was limited to milk and other farming requirements, helped by tourism in the early years. In the early 1930's the creamery at Ecton, a major user of the railway, closed, and most of the tourists went elsewhere. The railway quietly expired in 1934. Throughout its life the company had just two steam locomotives, built in Leeds but of 'Indian' appearance.

Wettonmill is a former mill site at a point where a minor road crosses the dale, climbing steeply on each side.

The café at Wettonmill

The Walk

Set off along the hard surfaced former railway line, heading up the valley (north) from Weag's Bridge, the track staying close to the (dry) riverbed below. Pass along the lower fringe of Ladyside Wood.

A high limestone pinnacle comes into view on the right. Thor's Cave is situated on its far side.

1. Reach a junction with information board.

The track to the right crosses a bridge before rising steeply up to the Cave.

Continue along the trackbed. Cross a bridge, which carried the

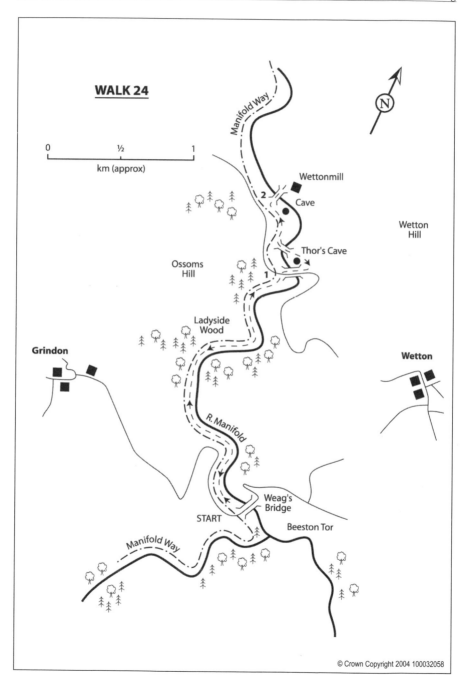

WALK 24

0   ½   1
km (approx)

Manifold Way

Wettonmill

2

Cave

Wetton
Hill

Thor's Cave

Ossoms
Hill

1

Ladyside
Wood

Grindon

Wetton

R. Manifold

Weag's
Bridge

START

Beeston Tor

Manifold Way

© Crown Copyright 2004 100032058

railway over the riverbed and join a minor public road. At this point, there is a choice of routes to Wettonmill. Both are public roads. The old railway track, straight on, is slightly more direct, crossing the riverbed again. Approach Wettonmill, cross Hoo Brook, then turn right to cross the river – now with water! – by a stone bridge into the Wettonmill complex, which has public conveniences in addition to the catering.

2. Return to Weag's Bridge by the same route, possibly using the alternative road from Wettonmill.

25. Ilam Hall

Distance: 5km (3 miles)

Total ascent: 60m (197ft)

Start/car parking: Large (pay) car park, with public conveniences and snack bar at the south end of Dovedale, grid reference 146509, accessed via Ilam or Thorpe.

Refreshments: Café operated by the National Trust at Ilam Hall. Snack bar at car park.

Map: 'White Peak' as for walk 5.

About the Walk

A gentle walk, partially circular, around the Ilam estate, with a link across fields to and from the bottom end of Dovedale. The total ascent is very modest, with no prolonged or steep sections. Very good paths, with few stiles. Minimal roadside walking.

Background

Of monastic origin, the Ilam estate was taken by Henry VIII on dissolution. It was then sold to John Port,

Footpath sign, Ilam

remaining with his family until 1809, when it was sold to David Pike-Watts. Pike-Watts's son in law, Jesse Watts-Russell had the house rebuilt, on a grand scale, by the architect James Trubshawe between 1821 and 1826. The stable block, now housing the café, is believed to be the only surviving part of the earlier house.

Also in the early 19th century, the gardens were much developed. The present Italian Gardens are the upper part of what was a much larger area descending in terraces from the house to the river. The 'pepper pot' tower, by the approach to the house, was built by Trubshawe as a dovecote.

The Church of the Holy Cross is originally of the 12th century, restored in 1618, then enlarged at the time of Jesse Watts-Russell by the addition of the unusual octagonal mausoleum, housing the marble monument to David Pike-Watts. The font is claimed to be Saxon, with carvings of scenes from the life of St Bertram. In the churchyard are two Saxon crosses.

The St Bertram legend claims that the hermit spent the latter years of his life in a small grotto in the bank of the River Manifold, taking drinking water from a nearby well, now within a walled enclosure. Higher up the hillside, above the grotto, is another shallow cave, equipped with a stone table and bench where, as a youth of nineteen, William Congreve (1690-1729) is believed to have written one of his stage comedies.

At the road junction outside the grounds of the hall is a striking monument to the wife of Jesse Watts-Russell.

Most of the Hall was demolished in the late 1920s. The remaining portion was purchased by Sir Robert McDougall and presented to the National Trust for use as a youth hostel. The Trust owns and manages the Park, with shop, information centre and café.

The Walk

Leave the car park by the vehicular entrance, cross the road and go through a gate/stile opposite, signposted 'public footpath to Ilam'. Bear left for 50m.

1. Turn right, uphill, along a path with rudimentary steps, reaching a double stile in 60m. Continue across a meadow, still rising along a faint path, aiming 40m to the right of the Izaak Walton Hotel. (the shapely hill behind is Thorpe Cloud). Go over a waymarked stile in a stone wall, followed by another in 40m, with an old footpath sign. Descend gently over grass towards Ilam; go through a kissing gate and continue. Bunster Hill is to the right. Go over a stile beside a gate, with Ilam Hall now in view. Go to the left to descend to a gate giving access to the public road.

2. Turn right, along the side of the road, by the river, to a road junction at the Watts-Russell monument. Turn right, then turn left in a little more than 100m along the Ilam Hall approach roadway, forking left again in 20m. In a further 30m turn left through a gate

signposted 'footpath to church and Hall'. The footpath leads straight to the church.

The outside doorway of the St Bertram's Chapel portion of the building has old inscriptions over the lintel. Built in 1618, the chapel has been a place of pilgrimage.

3. From the church continue initially towards the hall, but turn left to walk close to the boundary of the churchyard, heading for St Bertram's Bridge. Just before the bridge, there is a stone-walled water supply said to have been used by the Saint. Continue to the sharp, pointed bridge, restored in 1839.

4. Do not cross the bridge; turn right to walk over grass to the start of the 'Paradise Walk', a lovely track soon squeezed between river and rock, passing the tiny caves. Above, up a steep little path, is the 'Congreve' cave. Noticeable in the river are the 'Hamps Spring boil holes' where the underground waters of the River Manifold, which disappear close to Wettonmill, seven miles upstream, reappear. Pass the 'Battle Stone', which commemorates a conflict between Danes and Saxons, and carry on to a gate/stile, approximately half a mile from the bridge.

Hinkley Wood, across the river, has many specimens of lime trees, both small- and large-leaved varieties.

5. Turn sharp right to rise beside a fence. Close to the top of the rise the track bears to the left, across parkland, with many fine trees and Thorpe Cloud an impressive sight ahead. Pass a caravan site to the left, go through a gate and pass a 'visitor facilities' sign to reach the buildings of Ilam Hall.

The 'Manifold Tea Rooms' and the Italian Garden are to the right.

Continue through the arch, pass the youth hostel, then the 'pepper pot' to descend along the access roadway, joining the outward route to return to the car park.

If a return without ascent is preferred, stay with the little road, turning left at the road junction by the Izaak Walton Hotel entrance. From here there is a roadside footpath back to the car park.

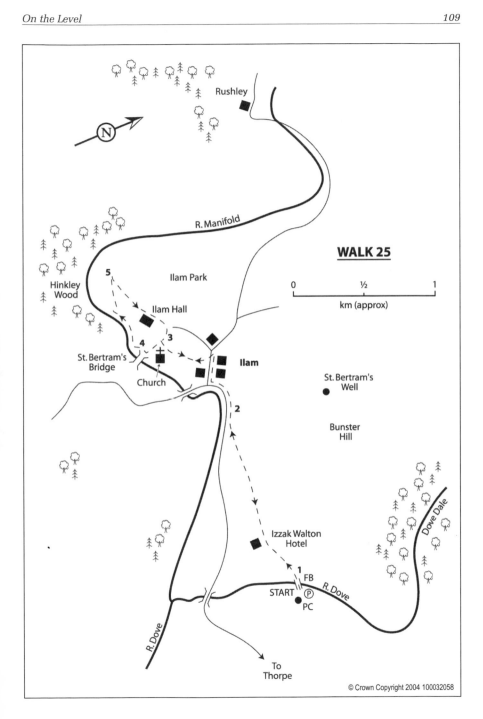

Rushley

R. Manifold

WALK 25

0 ½ 1
km (approx)

Ilam Park

Ilam Hall

Hinkley
Wood

St. Bertram's
Bridge

Church

Ilam

St. Bertram's
Well

Bunster
Hill

Dove Dale

Izzak Walton
Hotel

FB

START

PC

R. Dove

R. Dove

To
Thorpe

26. Dovedale

Distance: 3km (1¾ miles) – see below for other options.

Total ascent: 30m (98ft)

Start/car parking: Large (pay) car park with public conveniences and snack bar at entrance to Dovedale, grid reference 146509. Accessed via Ilam or Thorpe.

Refreshments: Snack bar at car park.

Map: 'White Peak' as for walk 5.

About the Walk

All walkers, 'level' or otherwise will want to enjoy a ramble along at least some of the delectable Dovedale. This basic route, out and back to the point where the track rises quite sharply at Lover's Leap, is a lovely undemanding stroll, passing some of the features which make the dale famous. If the turning point is at the foot of the rise, even that modest ascent can be avoided. Entirely easy underfoot.

An even shorter option is to cross the river on the stepping stones (easy except at very high water) and to return along the other side of the river, 1.5km (1 mile).

A longer option is to continue along the excellent path as far as Milldale, 5km (3 miles) passing all the well-known features, but doubling the total ascent if a return is made by the same route. However, from Milldale there is a minibus service (school terms only) back to the car park – the telephone number is displayed at the car park public conveniences. National Trust information about refreshments and public conveniences are available at Milldale.

Background

Dovedale has long been the best known of the popular dales, with easy public access. Indeed, at Bank Holidays and other peak periods its popularity may well deter those who like to enjoy nature without sharing it with the multitude. Lover's Leap, Tissington Spires, Jacob's Ladder, Reynard's Cave and Pickering Tor are just some of the features which contribute to the attraction of this lovely valley. The generous clothing of woodland does mean that some of the

The stepping stones in Dovedale

magnificent rock scenery reveals itself only to those who look quite carefully.

For walkers continuing to Milldale, the section above the junction with Hall Dale is more open.

The Walk

Start by passing between the Log Cabin and the public conveniences, along a path by the side of the river, soon passing the 'Izaak Walton Gauging Station – measuring the flow since 1969'. Reach a cattle grid and the roadway up to the stepping stones.

1. Turn right here and cross the footbridge over the river. Turn left along a path which hugs the edge of the water, with the steep slopes of Thorpe Cloud to the right.

2. Reach the famous stepping stones.

    A path to the right rises along Lin Dale, with an option, not for level walkers, to climb to the top of Thorpe Cloud. The very short walk crosses the stepping-stones, returning along the roadway on the far side of the river.

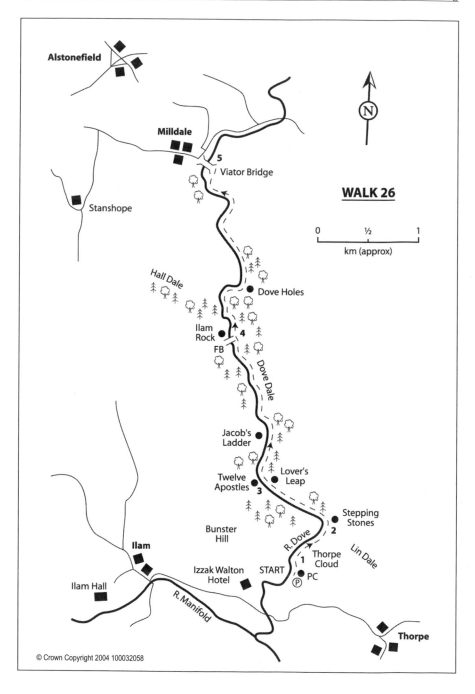

Alstonefield

Milldale

5

Viator Bridge

Stanshope

WALK 26

0   ½   1

km (approx)

Hall Dale

Dove Holes

Ilam
Rock   4

FB

Dove Dale

Jacob's
Ladder

Twelve   Lover's
Apostles   Leap
         3

Bunster   Stepping
Hill   Stones
                  2

Ilam   R. Dove   Lin Dale

Izzak Walton   START   Thorpe
Hotel   Cloud
                  1
Ilam Hall   P   PC

         R. Manifold

                        Thorpe

Otherwise, go through the double squeezer stile, passing a National Trust 'Dovedale' stile, and continue along the broad track along the bottom of the dale.

3. By the foot of the rise to Lover's Leap, the track veers away from the river, climbing quite steeply, with some steps, to a rock platform.

   The foot of the rise is the limit for a truly 'level' walk. However, for those with time and energy, the viewpoint at the top is well worth the extra effort.

   If continuing to Milldale, descend back to river level and stay with the clear path.

4. Pass a footbridge and junction of paths by Ilam Rock, then the junction with Hall Dale, followed by the huge caverns of Dove Holes.

5. Reach the tiny hamlet of Milldale, over the ancient packhorse 'Viator Bridge'. Return by the same route or use the (limited) bus service.

27. Tissington

Distance: 4.5km (2¾ miles)

Total ascent: 47m (154ft)

Start/car parking: Pay and display parking, with picnic tables, small shop and public conveniences, at the site of the former Tissington railway station, grid reference 178521. The car park is the focal point of the Tissington Trail and is signposted in Tissington village.

Refreshments: Old Coach House tea rooms in Tissington village.

Map: 'White Peak' as for walk 5.

About the Walk

A circuit which traverses Tissington village before crossing farm-land on generally good paths. The ascent is continuous for some distance but is all at easy gradients. The return uses part of the well-known Tissington Trail, along the trackbed of the former Buxton to Ashbourne railway line.

Background

Tissington has all the ingredients of a fine Peak District village – stone-built houses, a pond, a spacious green and an Elizabethan manor house.

Perhaps its greatest claim to fame is as the place of origin of the distinctive 'well-dressing' ceremonies, which are now an estab-lished part of life in many Peak District towns and villages. Tissington has several wells; the 'dressing' consists of the painstak-ing construction of religious tableaux, using flowers as the principal material. Although the origins of well dressing are rooted in giving thanks to pagan gods for supplies of life-giving water, following the revival of the ceremony in 1758 it has become entirely Christian. The Vicar holds a religious service on Ascension Day, processing to each well in turn, with hymns, psalms and a blessing.

The parish church, opposite the Hall, has many Norman features, including a fine chancel arch. The 19th-century north aisle was built in the Norman style. Members of the Fitzherbert family, occupiers of

Tissington Hall

the Hall for more than four centuries, have a distinctive monument at one end of the chancel arch.

Tissington Hall is open during the afternoon for a limited season as a visitor attraction.

The London and North Western Railway Company (LNWR) built their single track line from Buxton to Ashbourne late in the railway age. It was opened in 1899. Although the northern end of the line served large quarries close to Buxton, there was never much through traffic and the appeal to passengers in this sparsely populated area was likewise limited. In the competitive situation in the 1960's closure was inevitable. Hartington to Ashbourne was closed in 1963, Buxton to Hartington lingering until 1967.

Designation of much of the trackbed as the Tissington Trail, open to walkers, cyclists and horse riders, followed within a few years of closure.

The Walk

Walk up the access road to leave the car park. Join the public road, turning left. Bear left at the road junction in 30m. Pass a small green on the right and a duck pond on the left.

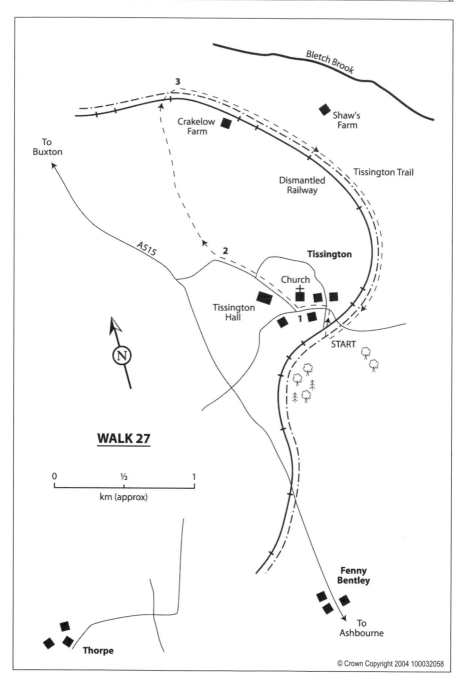

Bletch Brook

3

Shaw's
Farm

Crakelow
Farm

To
Buxton

Tissington Trail

Dismantled
Railway

A515

2

Tissington

Church

Tissington
Hall

1

START

N

WALK 27

0   ½   1

km (approx)

Fenny
Bentley

To
Ashbourne

Thorpe

© Crown Copyright 2004 100032058

1. At a triangular junction turn right to continue along the main village thoroughfare, rising gently.

   St Mary's church is up the bank to the right. The Old Coach House tea room is to the left.

   Pass Hall Well and then Tissington Manor, carrying on to the top edge of the village. Keep left at a junction, still rising, into farming countryside.

2. As the road bends to the left, climbing more steeply, turn right into a grass surfaced walled lane, still slightly uphill. Go through/over a gate/stile and cross a very large rough pasture, close to a wall on the left. After another gate/stile continue along the left edge of another large rough pasture. At the top of the rise is another section of lane, probably an old drove-way.

   There are now some excellent views across the valley of the Bletch Brook.

   Keep to the left edge of a meadow, by a wall, starting to descend, soon between walls again. Cross another meadow to a gate/stile and the trackbed of the former railway line.

   The line is surprisingly high above the valley bottom, with views across to Parwich Hill and the distinctive, but more distant, Minninglow with its crown of trees – the site of a Neolithic burial chamber.

3. Turn right. The return route is entirely straightforward, with plenty of bramble lining the way. Just before passing under a stone bridge there is a glimpse of the substantial Crakelow Farm, up to the right. Pass through a rock cutting and under two more bridges to reach the car park.

28. Cromford and the Canal

Distance: 6km (3¾ miles)

Total ascent: 80m (263ft)

Start/car parking: Large car park at Arkwright's Mill, grid reference 299570, or pay and display on the opposite side of the road. Signposted from the A6 below Cromford village. Bus services through Cromford include the 213/214, Sheffield to Wirksworth and the 411, Ashbourne to Matlock.

Refreshments: Café at the Arkwright's Mill complex.

Map: 'White Peak' as for walk 5.

About the Walk

The towpath of the Cromford Canal provides the outward part of this circular walk. The return along the valley side involves some ascent, principally a steady rise through woodland on an old packhorse trail. The final section of almost half a mile is along the side of a minor road.

Background

Arkwright's Mill at Cromford was the first successful water-powered cotton mill, extended from time to time to form the large complex seen today. Little by little, restoration is taking place, with the intention of creating a substantial visitor attraction.

The Cromford Canal was opened in 1793, primarily to serve this mill and other nearby industries. The canal connected with the River Trent, via the Erewash Canal. In 1830, the best known of all 'canal railways' – the Cromford and High Peak – was partially opened, eventually creating a link over the high and extensive upland of the Peak District between the Peak Forest Canal at Whaley Bridge and the Cromford Canal. At the Cromford end huge inclined planes were required to overcome the great difference in altitude between the upland railway and the low-lying canal. In 1853, the Cromford end of the railway was connected at High Peak Junction to the railway, which became the Midland main line. The importance of the canal then declined steadily.

By the side of the canal, the former Leawood pumping station, with its distinctive chimney, has been restored. The steam engine, of 1849, was used to raise water from the nearby River Derwent to feed the canal. On a few weekends throughout the year, the engine is still steamed as a visitor attraction.

The Walk

Start at the old buildings of Cromford Wharf, across the road from the Mill car park, and walk along the former towpath, soon passing a signpost 'Ambergate 5 miles'.

1. Reach High Peak Junction, with its modest visitor facilities including a shop, information and public conveniences, which are all accessed by crossing the swing bridge over the canal.

Leawood pumping station

The foot of the great inclined planes is reached behind the buildings.

Continue along the towpath, passing the old transhipment buildings on the far side of the water, then Leawood pumping station. Cross the aqueduct, which carries the canal over the River Derwent.

2. Turn left at a waymarked signpost 'Lea Bridge ½ mile'. Fork left at once into woodland, on the towpath of the long defunct Lea Bridge branch canal. Cross a bridge over the railway line, which itself crosses the river and disappears into a tunnel. Carry on through the woods, high above the river with the dry bed of the canal on the right. Go over a paved area, passing a house and what appears to have been the edge of a small wharf. Seventy metres after the house turn left along a waymarked path between walls. Join a lane by a stream. Turn right to reach a public road in 40m beside Lea Wood Cottage. Turn right to walk along the road-side footpath, rising gently past the Lea Wood boundary sign for 150m.

3. Turn left into a lane just before the entrance to John Smedley Ltd/Lea Mills. Go left at once through a squeezer stile and rise steadily through woodland, largely silver birch, on a good path. There is some stone paving, consistent with packhorse use.

    Distant views from here include Cromford village.

    At the top of the rise there is a decrepit wall on the right. Leave the wood between old gateposts, along a lane between stone walls. Pass a house – Sunny Bank – and join a drive by a signpost.

4. Turn left, downhill, on a surfaced roadway.

    Rugby fields are now prominent below.

    Pass the end of the drive leading to Bow Wood. In a further 100m turn right, over a stile with 'public footpath' sign, to follow a path initially rising across rough pasture, leading to a squeezer stile. Continue across the next rough pasture, rising very gently on a clear path, passing a stone trough on the right. By the end of an old stone wall bear right, uphill, with the remains of the wall and an outgrown hedge on the left; there is a waymark on a post 40m from the end of the wall. Carry on to a waymarked stile and enter woodland. The path is narrow but reasonably clear. Go through a squeezer stile at the far end, at a junction of paths.

5. Turn left to descend a steep little path at the edge of the wood,

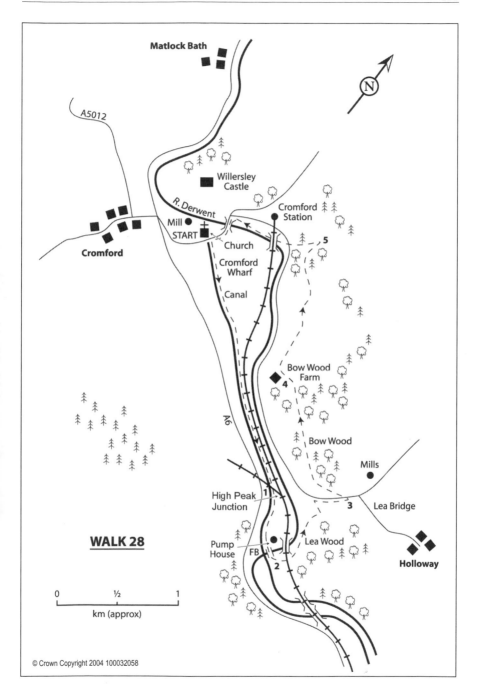

Matlock Bath

A5012

Willersley
Castle

R. Derwent

Cromford
Station

Mill ●
START
Cromford
Church
Cromford
Wharf

Canal

5

Bow Wood
Farm
4

A6

Bow Wood

Mills

High Peak
Junction
1

3
Lea Bridge

WALK 28

Pump
House
FB

Lea Wood

2

Holloway

0   ½   1

km (approx)

© Crown Copyright 2004 100032058

helped by steps and some artificial surface. Go over a waymarked stile to join a public road. Turn right to walk by the roadside, under a railway viaduct and past the end of the station approach road. Pass the entrance to Willersley Castle (Arkwright's former home) before crossing Cromford Bridge over the river, passing St Mary's church and returning to the car park.

More Leisure, Less Pressure!

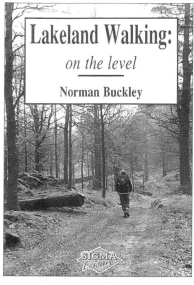

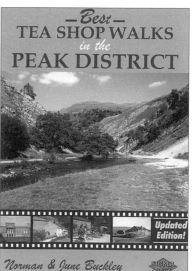